D0052502

A
CHICKEN'S GUIDE
TO TALKING TURKEY
WITH YOUR KIDS
ABOUT SEX

A
CHICKEN'S GUIDE
to TALKING TURKEY
WITH YOUR KIDS
ABUT SEX

DR. KEVIN LEMAN
KATHY FLORES BELL

ZONDERVAN®

ZONDERVAN.com/
AUTHORTRACKER
follow your favorite authors

A Chicken's Guide to Talking Turkey with Your Kids about Sex
Copyright © 2004 by Dr. Kevin Leman and Kathy Flores Bell

This title is also available in a Zondervan audio edition.
Visit www.zondervan.fm.

Requests for information should be addressed to:

Zondervan, *Grand Rapids, Michigan* 49530

This Edition: 978-0-310-28350-8

Library of Congress Cataloging-in-Publication Data

Leman, Kevin.
    A chicken's guide to talking turkey with your kids about sex. / Kevin Leman and Kathy
Flores Bell. 1st ed.
      p. cm.
    Includes bibliographical references and index.
    ISBN 978-0-310-25096-8 (hardcover)
    1. Sex instruction. 2. Puberty. 3. Sexual ethics. 4. Parenting.
  I. Bell, Kathy Flores, 1958– II. Title.
  HQ57.L46 2004
  649'.65–dc22   2003023109

All Scripture quotations, unless otherwise indicated, are taken from the *Holy Bible, New International Version*®. NIV®. Copyright © 1973, 1978, 1984 by International Bible Society. Used by permission of Zondervan. All rights reserved.

Internet addresses (websites, blogs, etc.) and telephone numbers printed in this book are offered as a resource to you. These are not intended in any way to be or imply an endorsement on the part of Zondervan, nor do we vouch for the content of these sites and numbers for the life of this book.

All rights reserved. No part of this publication may be reproduced, stored in a retrieval system, or transmitted in any form or by any means—electronic, mechanical, photocopy, recording, or any other—except for brief quotations in printed reviews, without the prior permission of the publisher.

Interior design by Michelle Espinoza

Printed in the United States of America

09 10 11 12 13 14 · 21 20 19 18 17 16 15 14 13 12 11 10 9 8 7 6 5 4 3

This first book is dedicated to my four remarkable moms: my birth mother, Gloria Flores, who loves "big as the sky and deep as the ocean"; Diana Comaduran, CFNP, who will always be my second mom; Dr. Mary Adam—she is "Jama" and I am "Newsweek"; and, of course, beautiful Aunt Barb—Barbara Tompkins.

—Kathy Flores Bell

To Lauren Leman,
My little gift from God.

You pulled off one of the great upsets of all time when you were born to two very surprised parents who were both pushing fifty. But God, with his infinite wisdom, knew you'd be our fifth child, and I can't imagine our family without you, our youngest born.

Lauren, I'm so proud to be your daddy. You have wisdom far beyond your years; your love and your insight into human nature amazes me (like the time you said you were glad to be a girl because it's easier to be good when you're a girl); your sweet spirit, gentle ways, and compassionate nature have helped your older sisters and brother not just to put up with you but to genuinely adore you. I know they'll always be there for you, even when I'm dribbling drool on my walker in the old folks' home!

If there's ever a day when I can't say it myself, I hope you can read it here and never forget: you'll always be Daddy's little muffin. There will never be another one like you, nor a father-daughter story quite like ours.

—Kevin Leman

Contents

Acknowledgments

One phone call changed my life. Kay Lindley wanted to do a radio show about menstruation and knew that my mother had used a Ziploc bag and other kitchen items to teach me about "the birds and the bees." Now it was my turn to pass on to radio listeners what my mom and dad had taught me. That alone was remarkable, since they were "irresponsible" teen parents who raised four kids and had little education and no money. Thus, Kevin Leman and I met on the radio over ten years ago.

I want to thank Kay Lindley for listening to the Holy Spirit and insisting that puberty issues are crucial for parents to discuss. Thanks to my parents, who are incredible people, for grooming me into an innovative teacher by their example and support, and to Diana Comaduran, RNP, who created an internship for me at the local clinic, where I worked with numerous teen moms while I was still in high school myself. Thanks to Luz Elena Shearer, who insisted that I attend a natural family planning conference to become a better sexuality educator, and to my husband, Mike, my devoted spouse and Sacrament, who funded my efforts and fueled the opportunity to develop my style and specific techniques that are in this first book. Touché to my first fifth-grade class of boys—my son in attendance—at St. Cyril's Catholic School, who had to endure my "on-the-job" training, and to Sr. St. Joan and Sr. Mary Kevin Ford at Carondelet Health Network for allowing me to fly as a volunteer at St. Joseph's Hospital. To my gem of a secretary, Donna Pexa, I am grateful for your love through it all, for keeping an eye on me and my ever-stressed pulse.

Thanks to Jan Howard and Connie Teeple, who encouraged me, nudged me, and slapped me upside the head to focus; to Dr. Mary Adam, who bravely volunteered her services to help me pull off mother-daughter programs and even more bravely nailed me on medical accuracy; to Laurel Krinke, public school teacher, who beautifully augmented my work with learning activities; and to beautiful Aunt Barb, Barb Tompkins—God love her—who introduced me to the world of character education. What would I have done without you, Barb?

A special hug and thanks goes out to my in-laws, Jack and Dolores Bell, who just happened to be in town when Kevin asked me to get chapters ready—they cooked and cleaned and taxied kids without a second thought; and to my children—John "Boy," Amy "Rebecca," Elizabeth "Lizzie-Bear," Alicia "Peanut Butter," and Nettie, our "adopted" daughter—who rolled with the punches as I raced through deadlines and numerous drives to Kevin's house, Kinko's, or the post office to get drafts in on time. And I would be remiss if I neglected the hospital staff at University Medical Center—those wonderful hematology-oncology nurses who allowed me to set up an office while Lizzie transfused, so I wouldn't miss a beat on the home front and with this book.

I cannot neglect our editor, John Sloan, one detailed kind of guy, without whose talent and time this book would have never come to life. Last, but not least, my thanks to Gary Thomas and Dave Greene, whose brilliant minds, sacred hands, and holy wisdom pastorally married my comprehensive, character-based human sexuality education with Kevin's marriage and family material. For the zillions of hours they spent talking on the phone, listening to tapes, reading articles, and compiling research, I am forever indebted and grateful.

And to the Holy Spirit, lest I forget, this is not my project but yours.

—Kathy Flores Bell

Chapter 1

It's a Tough Job, but Someone Has to Do It

It marked the beginning of yet another childrearing era in the Leman household when my daughter asked me, "Dad, can I have a party?"

"What kind of party?" I asked.

"Oh," she said nonchalantly, "a Christmas party."

"Sounds good to me," I said. "Who are you going to invite?"

"Allison, Kristen, Katey Jo, Lindsey, Corey, Crystal, Amy . . ."

I knew all these names, so I only half listened, but suddenly I caught on to a very pregnant pause. Hannah looked at me uncertainly, then added a little more quickly, "and maybe Chris, Michael, Kyle, Ben, Mark, and Josh."

I stopped what I was doing and looked at Hannah, seeing for the first time that curious twilight I had witnessed in my older daughters—a girl's slow but steady passage into womanhood.

Though Hannah was fourteen years old, I couldn't help thinking, *Holy crow, I don't know whether I want that or not. Boys and girls at the same party, huh? So we're at that stage, are we?*

Suddenly I felt whisked back to when I was twelve years old and the swirling sensations of one puberty-laden night on the school dance floor. I was in seventh grade, and I remember dancing *ever so closely* to Wendy Winfield at the Broomstick Bounce. I distinctly recall what she looked like that night, the red crewneck sweater she wore, even the song we danced to ("In the Still of the Night")—and that was nearly half a century ago!

I can't believe this, I remember thinking as Wendy and I danced, *I'm holding on to a girl.* Two years earlier I had hated girls; I either wanted to play practical jokes on them or avoid them altogether. Yet there I was dancing with one, and liking it!

What is happening to me? I wondered.

Remember those days? Can you bring to mind the first inkling that you "liked" someone? When was the first time you asked a friend to find out whether someone liked you as much as you liked him? When did you first receive a note passed between desks or at your locker between classes and felt your heart pounding so hard that you were sure the school band could march to its rhythm?

Take a trip down memory lane; it will be helpful as you face your child's passage through the precious season of life we call puberty. At the start of that season, nothing seems as gross as kissing a member of the opposite sex; at the end, nothing sounds so sweet. We want to help you become your child's most trusted guide as he or she passes through puberty.

A Book of Firsts

Your eight- and nine-year-old kids may not be saying a lot about sex, but they're probably thinking about it. At ten and eleven, they're likely to be talking about it with their friends. Unfortunately, at twelve, thirteen, and fourteen, if you haven't been involved in their lives, they may be *having* sex.

As central as the message "abstain from sex" is, it's merely a one-liner if *you're* abstaining from talking openly with your kids about their sexuality, one of God's greatest gifts. We're sexual beings from day one, and kids ask questions all along the way. Who better for them to learn the answers from than you, their parents?

This is a book about puberty, that time in your child's life between the ages of eight and fourteen, and the firsts that accompany it: first bra, first period, first Little League supporter and cup, first discussion about your child's development and expected behavior with the opposite sex. Anyone who deals with a pubescent child between third and eighth grade—parents (married and single); schoolteachers, counselors, and nurses; and grandparents—will benefit from this book. It will help you moms buy that first cup for your son in Little League and help you dads navigate the feminine-hygiene aisle at the supermarket and buy that first bra for your daughter. It is a book for anyone who wants to be prepared to address the physical, emotional, and spiritual components of a child's questions.

Whether the years you've already had with your child have been wonderful or challenging, we want to give you the skills you'll need to complete the job of guiding them from being kids to being mature young men and women.

At the very start, we want to commend you for taking the time and making the effort to become better informed and better equipped. So many parents take the ostrich approach, burying their heads in the sand while they hope their children come out okay.

That's flat-out dangerous. As soon as your children hit puberty, they are actively thinking about their bodies, talking about sex, and sorting through the conflicting messages they get from their peers and society. If you leave them to do this on their own, you're abandoning them to the lure of their hormones, the seduction of false and twisted information, and the painful reality of inappropriate sexual activity.

An Ongoing Process

Parents often ask us when to start talking about sex, but sex education—or better stated, puberty education—is an ongoing process if you're doing the job correctly. If you reduce this education process to simply having "a talk," you're missing the point. Being close enough to your child to talk meaningfully about sex is more about nurturing an ongoing, open, loving relationship than having a onetime discussion. Kids today need this from parents as urgently as ever.

Here's an example of what we're talking about: the success we have in talking about sex with our kids is heavily influenced by how we handle the other changes happening in their bodies and by the openness we cultivate with them in general. A common mistake that many parents make is to focus on the "bathing suit" areas of the body when approaching "the topic."

Can we make a suggestion? The best way to begin opening the doors of conversation is to focus on the neck-up issues of preadolescence, the area many kids refer to as "first base." Both of us have seen many kids who frankly feel shocked when their previously silent parents suddenly start talking about issues "below the belt"—the "third base" and "home plate" regions for kids. These moms and dads haven't earned their children's confidence, but in a desperate attempt to make up for lost time, they stumble through an embarrassing "talk." The end result usually feels uncomfortable for both parent and child.

During early puberty, kids focus far more time and attention on the neck up, and by spending time with them on these seeming crises—keeping zits at bay, bad-hair days, cracking voices, and their cursed clumsiness—you'll establish openness, a track record, and the confidence to face together the more intimate discussions: what exactly sexual intercourse is, how to journey through a world that trumpets condoms as the answer to everything, and why to wait for marriage to have sex.

The best thing you can do for a preadolescent is to show empathy with that first embarrassing pimple or cold sore. Take it seriously, drive them to the drugstore, and get the appropriate over-the-counter medicine. Show them how to style their hair when it's sticking up; talk to them about bad breath and flaky scalps. When your children learn to rely on you for these things, it will be natural for them to rely on you when other issues arise: the first period, the first nocturnal emission, the first time a young girl notices that a boy she's with has an erection.

Neck-up issues are a parent's best way to make many valuable deposits for the future. Don't minimize your children's pain with statements like: "Don't worry, honey, nobody can see that pimple." "Don't you care about anything besides your hair?" "What's your problem, honey? It's not the end of the world; it's just a cold sore!" When you talk like this, you teach your child that you don't care, you don't empathize, and if they want a sympathetic ear, they'd better call a friend.

Here's the real challenge: physical maturity does not equal emotional or relational maturity. When kids reach puberty it is time to talk to them about sexuality, yes, but what sets pubescent kids up for success in their sexuality is character education, personal hygiene, and regular communication with their parents. It is these basic skills—how to care for changing skin and hair, how to *wait* for that video game they really want, how to communicate openly with their parents when they hear the f-word from their peers and wonder what it means—that make kids receptive when their parents begin talking to them about abstaining from sex before marriage.

Early puberty, the fourth and fifth grades, is the time to help kids cultivate these basic hygiene skills—before the hormones kick in. By sixth grade, the hormones are toggled to *on* in many kids, and by the seventh and eighth grades, kids are moving into the adolescent years, a landscape dominated by hormones.

We all grow up, and just as you made it through puberty, your son or daughter will pass through it as well. Earlier we asked you to take stock of the feelings you had during puberty. Pause once again and consider what your parents did right, as well as what they did wrong. If puberty was a tough time for you, what might they have done to make it easier? What type of things built a wall between you and your parents? Is there anything they did that was particularly helpful?

Remember: now *you're* the parent, making the same choices your parents made while you were off dancing at the Broomstick Bounce.

Let's begin by looking at the telltale wake-up calls that become familiar to every parent.

Wake-Up Calls

Little John Bell was just five years old when we visited a farm, where we watched a cow and her calf in the pasture.

"Momma," John asked me as we stood there, "how did that baby cow get inside that mommy's tummy?"

"God made it in a special place," I began, "and then that baby cow grew and grew for a really long time before finally coming out one day."

I looked at the calf. "And there it is," I concluded, satisfied I'd given him a good, spiritual, though admittedly vague, biological answer.

"No, Momma," John said, "I want to know *how* it got in there."

"Well," I continued, "the mommy has an egg and the daddy has a seed, and when the two of them got together that made the baby calf. See the brown skin of that cow there and the white skin of that one over there?" I said as I began giving him an introductory genetics lesson.

John looked me straight in the eyes. "*No*, Momma," he said, "I want to know *how* that baby cow got into that momma cow."

There is a time for skirting around the issue and there is a time for straightforwardness, and clearly we had passed from one to the other. "Do you really want to know?" I asked.

"Yeah," he said, "I want to know."

I had already taught John the body parts, so I said, "That daddy cow over there has a penis, and he put it inside the mommy cow's vagina. He released his seed, which traveled up into that mommy to meet her egg. That's how it started forming the little baby calf inside her, the calf that's right there in the field now."

He looked at the calf. "That's *really* gross," he said. He stood there quietly, staring intently at the calf, and then looked up at me. "Is that what you and Dad had to do to get me?" he asked.

I looked down at him. "Yeah."

"Yuck!" he exclaimed.

I have yet to meet the parent of a fourth grader who is excited to begin closing the chapter on childhood. There's something inherently sweet about a child's innocence, when boys get more excited catching frogs and garter snakes than they do catching furtive glimpses of Britney Spears and thinking about garter belts.

But as your child enters puberty, you'll begin to notice things your child says or does—subtle things that have never before seemed important to your child. During back-to-school shopping, your little boy suddenly cares what label his new shirt carries, when only the year before, he didn't care whether his clothes were even washed. One day your little girl is playing house with the doll your mother handed down to you, and the next she declares she's not interested in dolls, *period*. One evening you're watching a football game with your son and you notice his eyes lingering on the cheerleaders. He used to say "gross" when the camera panned that bouncing bunch, but his reverent silence and intense stare tell you that "gross" is the last thing he's thinking now.

These moments wake us up to something that has already happened. It's similar to opening the shades on a winter morning and seeing that your yard has been covered by an overnight arrival of snow. Sometime during the night, puberty arrived.

The signs aren't always obvious, of course. Your daughter isn't going to wake up one morning, sit down at breakfast, and say, "Hey, guess what? I hit puberty today!" Your son won't gather everyone's attention at dinner and announce, "I just want you all to know that I like girls now."

Biological clocks don't have alarms, and they aren't that precise. You have to know your child well enough to realize that when he begins meticulously combing his hair after a lifetime of being perfectly content with the hairstyle of a haystack, you've begun entering this wonderful, new phase of life.

You are right to pay attention to these wake-up calls, but don't panic; they're only wake-up calls. These changes were bound to happen and are signs that your son or daughter is moving toward adulthood. The temporary insanity of adolescence may seem just around the corner, but it's still years away.

Unfortunately, the world is making our job tougher every day.

The Critical Years

Both of us have worked with numerous families as they sought to make the transition from pubescence to adolescence. The one constant during this stretch of time is change. Kids who have behaved like normal, all-American children will begin showing sides of themselves you swear you've never seen.

One day your daughter hates chicken, and the next she eats four helpings of it. A simple pimple becomes a volcano, and a boundary you set becomes the beaches of Normandy. You may hear, "You *never* let me do this! You *never* let me do that!" in response to something that, to your recollection, has come up in conversation only once before.

We know of one mother who casually asked her adolescent daughter at dinner, "Did you finish your homework, honey?" and was met with an explosive, "You *hate* me, don't you? Why can't you just leave me alone?!"

Though puberty is a time when you may, for the first time, legitimately feel like killing your kid, it's also that critical time when you as a parent need to guide him or her through the stormy seas of life to that port we call adolescence. As a parent, you are the one who must navigate a semistraight line to help this child whose boat is being tossed on a sea of hormones and blown by the winds of culture, and the winds today have grown strong indeed.

Kids in this generation are growing up in a world in which we've traded Mathers. Jerry Mathers ("as the Beaver") has been replaced by foul-mouthed rapper Marshall Mathers (Eminem). We've gone from that baby-faced kid next door whose favorite saying was, "Gee, Wally!" to a guy whose latest album features vulgarly explicit lyrics. Kids are engaging in oral sex, not at parties or friends' homes when parents are away, but on *school buses* and at *school* during school hours—and many of them don't even consider it sex.

This isn't a problem limited to kids outside the church. In his book *Right from Wrong,* Josh McDowell cited a study that showed 27 percent of Christian teens had experienced sexual intercourse by the age of eighteen, and 55 percent had engaged in fondling breasts.[1]

It's a turbulent world our children are entering.

Can we be blunt? The raw reality of today's society, in which the vast majority of kids have sexual intercourse before the age of twenty, means that a passive approach to parenting will no longer work. If you do what many parents do—cross your fingers, hope for the best, and stay silent—your family will add to the statistics of out-of-wedlock pregnancies, sexually transmitted diseases, and broken hearts, all before your children reach the age of twenty-one.

What have you shared with your kid about life? Have you *really* discussed things, or have you avoided the difficult topics that need frank discussion the most?

Here's just one example: Mom, you have to come to grips with the fact that your son (and very likely your daughter) *will* masturbate. His body is beginning to produce semen at a very high rate, and there are only three ways that semen will come out: sexual intercourse, masturbation, or nocturnal emission. You can help him choose how he will handle this natural biological pressure, or you can simply avoid the topic and leave him to stumble onto a healthy approach all on his own.

In the same way, your daughter is going to become interested in guys. Whether these new connections are healthy or exploitive will depend in large part on how well she is prepared to handle older boys' interest. She can learn by trial and error, or she can benefit from a loving parent's advice and thus avoid considerable emotional trauma. Toward the end of puberty, as your child heads into adolescence, that little girl or boy who used to crawl up into your lap might be thinking about crawling into other people's laps.

The precious, critical years of puberty are over once the firsts are done: Your daughter is beyond the breast buds and has started her period. Your son has had his first nocturnal emission and, toward the end of puberty, begins moving into those emotional and psychological changes that accompany adolescence. But in early puberty, your son or daughter still straddles childhood and adolescence, a time some call the "tweenager" years.[2] During your child's puberty, you still have a great deal of influence by lovingly instructing your child and setting boundaries.

A Parent to Be Proud Of

Back in 1994, *USA Today*[3] chose an "all-USA high school baseball team" and asked each player several questions, including whom they most admired. A common theme came up in their responses. Among the players questioned, you may recognize many as current sports professionals:

Jaret Wright: "My father, Clyde."

Mark Johnson: "My father, George."

Derek Baker: "My father, Don."

Troy Glaus: "My mother, Karen Jensen."

Rob Hauswald: "My mother, Karen May."

Doug Million: "My father, Dave."

Josh Booty: "My father, John."

McKay Christensen: "My father, Stephen."

Ben Grieve: "My father, Tom."

Brian Shultz: "My father, Steve."

Every single player chose a parent as the person they most admire.

One of the problems both of us have with the way sexual education is presented in most schools is that too many educators act as if the most important thing a preadolescent needs is information.

That's not true. Information is important, but the most important thing a child needs to succeed is an involved and loving parent.

The fact that you picked up this book and have read this far tells us that you want to be that kind of a parent. Good for you. Now, let's get started!

Chapter 2

Parenting Pitfalls in Puberty

Why Parents Don't Talk about Sex

The stack depressed me.

I can't walk in the door and teach this, I (Kathy) thought as I sat on the floor of Waldenbooks. I was preparing to teach sexual education to fifth graders and had every available sex ed book open before me.

The kids had all the right questions: *Why am I the way I am? Why do I get so emotional? What is true love?* I knew this class was a wide-open door to address the changes they were going through. But I felt appalled by what I read and by what people considered appropriate for fifth-grade sexual education. One curriculum designed for pubescent kids had a little boy and girl holding hands on the cover and addressed such questions as "What is a first kiss?"

"Whoa, time out!" I wanted to scream. "Let's help kids figure out what's happening to their bodies rather than launching into matchmaker games!"

Both of us have met a lot of parents who wish they could call "Time out" at home, to somehow freeze their child before he or she gets any older. Wordly influences seem to press against kids' innocence when they are younger and younger. One mother openly worried about her adopted daughter: "I'm afraid that she's going to end up being pregnant before she's eighteen years old." As she surveyed the kids older than her daughter, she feared that sexual behavior seemed virtually inevitable. She had heard that many adopted kids used sex as a way to deal with issues of abandonment and betrayal, and she assumed her daughter might take that path as well.

"I want to help her avoid this trap," she confessed, "but I haven't a clue what to do to stop it." Her whole body slumped in the chair, signaling her early sense of defeat.

The daughter she described was just four years old.

It's sad, but many parents wear this sense of inevitable failure. They don't realize that they can begin helping their children "connect the dots" to success in their sexuality by using the concepts covered in this book. Of course, we can't *guarantee* that a child raised by these standards won't experiment sexually, but it's been our experience that children who have benefited from this approach are far less likely to engage in harmful, premarital sexual play.

At the other end of the spectrum are the hypervigilant parents who are as obsessed with succeeding as other parents are obsessed with the fear of failing. Have you ever watched a goalie at a soccer game? He remains ceaselessly wary, ready to take a dive when the ball comes sailing in. Parents can be like that when it comes to making sure their child will not turn out like the kids they read about. The sad thing is that many such parents spend so much time protecting their children that they neglect to prepare them. The kid isn't learning the skills to deal with what comes her way; she's simply being scared into compliance.

Such an approach may delay sexual experimentation, but it won't address the root causes. In fact, this type of home often creates the most sexually promiscuous children we see. In just a few short years, you won't be able to follow your daughter around. What will keep her focused when you're no longer playing goalie?

Parents must begin helping their children make the transition from the innocence of childhood to the reality of adulthood in appropriate ways. We're not saying it's easy. Since we have heard all the excuses, let's get those out of the way right now.

Shameful Silence

Nobody talked to you. Let's be honest: few of us had a healthy discussion with our parents about the explicit issues and desires of early sexual temptation and development. The vast majority of us had to stumble along in the dark and find our own way.

Because a healthy approach was never modeled for you, your attitude might go in one of two negative ways. You may think, *If I figured everything out, I guess they will, too.* Or you may be more subtle: *I don't have a clue what to say, so rather than say the wrong thing, maybe I should just remain silent.*

Do you want your kids to just get by, or do you want them to excel? Yeah, you made it, but think of the stress and uncertainty you faced having to figure everything out on your own. Is that the type of spiritual inheritance you want to leave your own children?

Some of you don't want to enter emotional territory that will painfully remind you of the help you wished you had received from your parents, but it's time to move on. Sticking your head in the sand and pretending your kid won't have to deal with these issues perpetuates a sad parental neglect. We can hide behind our parents' failure only for so long; someday we're going to have to start forging new patterns for the generations ahead.

Think about it this way: if you'll take the initiative, you have the opportunity to pave the way for your children, grandchildren, and even great-grandchildren. You're setting an example that can influence your family for generations to come.

You lack the skills, appropriate words, and confidence to say what needs to be said. Fair enough. If the problem is merely ignorance, that can be fixed, and you're fixing it by reading this book! None of us knew how to fill out tax forms the first time we filed our return, but because the government required us to file a return, we read books, we talked to knowledgeable people, and we got the information we needed to complete the task.

Parenting is no different. You're not born with the information you need, and depending on your parents, you may not have had good parenting modeled for you. Ignorance is curable; it's laziness and cowardice that tend to be fatal. You can overcome your lack of skills and knowledge, provided you remain willing to stretch yourself.

Since you've made the effort to read this book, we can safely assume that you're ready to take advantage of teachable moments. You're eager to follow through and will do so once you have the skills and direction you need. Good for you!

You're embarrassed about the body. Some of you may have come from a family that didn't talk about the body, and so the subject is altogether taboo in your mind. You can't even imagine saying the words "penis" and "vagina" to your kids and have in fact already resorted to such euphemisms as their "thing." When they took baths, you handed them a washcloth and said, "Don't forget to wash *down there.*"

For those parents who come from families embarrassed about the body, we recommend you first acknowledge that this is a difficult topic to discuss. It's difficult because it's deeply personal and because it's something you may not have had much practice talking about. We feel uncomfortable because many people have turned sex into something filthy.

This is your chance to communicate your beliefs and values to your kids as you talk about life and sex. What a tremendous opportunity to wrap your conversation in the context that sex is a wonderful gift from God!

You may tell your kid, "Quite frankly, I have a hard time talking about this. The reality is that I shouldn't be uncomfortable, because what I'm telling you is part of how wonderfully you were made." Tie your discussion back to your value system.

A part of every parent wants to keep his or her children under glass for life so that they don't get exposed to the evil out there. But by acknowledging the difficulty of talking about sex and then wrapping the conversation in your values, you'll overcome a culture that has degraded one of God's most precious gifts.

Embarrassment can be handled. Kathy has had to learn how to use precise names in front of snickering fifth graders, and Dr. Leman has even given a talk on sexual education to an entire assembly of students when his daughter sat among them! Love for your children and concern for their welfare should overcome any self-centered entanglements like embarrassment.

Other parents deal with their discomfort by joking about body parts and normal body functions, but never talk meaningfully about them. We're all for laughter; in the right context, a well-placed piece of humor can diffuse a lot of tension and really keep things going. But be aware that if *you* don't take these issues seriously, your children may not, either. And for them, the consequences of that are downright frightening.

You're afraid of appearing hypocritical because of your own sexual activity before marriage, so you avoid the subject out of shame. In our experience, this excuse is becoming more and more common. A couple getting married, with both of the partners virgins, is now sadly unusual, and the guilt caused by premarital sex is being passed down to future generations. *Because I failed,* the thinking goes, *I have no right to preach to anyone else.*

This is a false premise for parenting. In my (Dr. Leman's) book *Adolescence Isn't Terminal: It Just Feels Like It!* I talk about how I have freely shared with my children many of my embarrassments and failings as a youngster. This has created intimacy with my kids, not judgment. I happened to be a virgin when I got married, but I did a lot of other stupid stuff—smoking, pranks, that kind of thing.

We're not suggesting that you go into detail, but it's fine to say, "Honey, I've made some painful mistakes in this area, and that's why I want to help you learn from my failures." You are under no obligation to reveal any more than that; in fact, we recommend that you don't. Kids tend to see their parents as asexual beings to begin with, and they probably won't want to hear what their parents did and with whom.

Instead of using your experience as a jumping-off point, use one of the many examples that arise naturally in today's society. Here's how this works in the Leman household: as we write this, we learned that a girl who played basketball at my daughter's school has—at the age of sixteen—become pregnant. Goodbye, hoops! Not too many basketball shirts accommodate pregnant women.

My daughter saw the effect of an out-of-wedlock pregnancy, close-up. I like to use real-life examples such as these to remind my kids that God's laws really are perfect, and when we go outside these boundaries, we pay for it. I can't imagine any one of my daughters going from that conversation to, "So, Dad, did you and Wendy get it on at the Broomstick Bounce?"

What *is* helpful to include about your past? We think it's helpful for kids to know that, in general, when you were a kid you, too, had temptations or hassles with guys or girls—the same as what they are experiencing or will experience. You got through it and they will, too. If kids ask pointed questions such as, "Did you get through it perfectly?" you might answer, "Well, no, there are things I wish I could do over again." If you take it in stride, most kids will accept that.

If perfection were the requirement for teaching, we might as well pack it up and go home now! None of us have perfect pasts, but we're all called to turn our painful failures into teachable moments for our kids. Sooner or later, your kids are going to find out that you weren't perfect; any other thought is just plain fantasy. Avoiding difficult topics to delay the inevitable is foolish.

Remember: just because you *start* a conversation doesn't mean you need to fear losing control of it. You're the parent; you can determine how far the discussion goes. Keep the goal and purpose in mind: the two of you aren't getting together to discuss *your* sexual history, but rather to help your child create his or her own.

Prolonged naïveté. Isn't denial wonderful? It can keep us feeling happy and pleasant for days on end, but we're dancing on the railroad tracks when we adopt this device. Sooner or later, we're going to be flattened by a locomotive called reality.

Trying to keep your child a *child* for as long as you can is a noble plan. We both agree that we should keep our kids *kids;* the world tries to get them to grow up too fast. But human boys and girls are born with clocks ticking toward puberty and adolescence, and it is our duty to train them to deal with the world as it is, not as we wish it were. We can't keep our kids under glass. If we do, and then we turn them loose into the world at eighteen, they'll be sorely taken advantage of.

Perhaps some of you parents know how cruel the world can be from your own bad experiences. Naturally, you want to keep your kids from experiencing those things, which is good and right. But not telling them about what's in the world will not help them cope with it. That's why this book is about balance: what to say, when to say it, and how to say it.

Others of you have simply lived a very sheltered life. Some of you mothers may believe that your son will never have a nocturnal emission, also called a wet dream. We're telling you, he's *going* to have that wet dream. He can no more hold back those wet dreams than your daughter can hold back her menstrual periods. The question is, when he wakes up for the first time with a couple of ounces of good protein in his pajamas, do you want this to be a total surprise to him? Or do you want to take credit for telling him that it would happen? Your child needs a healthy understanding of the world, and how to make responsible, moral decisions is a critical skill to develop during this time.

So by all means, keep kids *kids,* but let young adults become young adults! In my (Dr. Leman's) practice, I've seen way too many dads purchase age-inappropriate gifts for their children. They buy their ten-year-old daughter a Disney doll when she wants a soccer ball. They look for cartoon T-shirts when their daughter would prefer a bracelet or earrings. One or two years may not make much difference in *your* outlook on life, but for an eight-year-old compared to a ten-year-old, and for a ten-year-old compared to a twelve-year-old, those twenty-four months can represent light years of development.

If you keep talking about things that your child left behind years ago, eventually he'll catch on and seek the answers to his toughest questions elsewhere.

You think that's what the school and church are for. Some parents find out that their kids are studying anatomy in health class at school and think, *Whew! Glad that's taken care of!* Then the parents hear that the youth minister at their church gave a single talk on abstinence and tragically assume that their kid has learned everything he or she needs to know.

School and church youth groups can be beneficial assistants when it comes to educating your children, but watch out if you expect them to be generals. I (Kathy) have spoken in many of these classes and can tell you that for every question I am asked and have answered, at least a dozen go untouched. Do you think your daughter's going to hold up her hand in front of her class and say, "Is something wrong with me if I have a period just ten days after the previous one stopped?" Do you think your son is going to ask what he's supposed to do if he suddenly gets an erection while he's getting undressed for gym class?

Besides, remember the books Kathy mentioned at the start of this chapter? If you allow someone else to become the primary sexual educator of your children, you're taking a big risk. Who knows whether they share your values and beliefs?

If this has been your approach in the past, you can still make changes. Begin by offering your child an apology.

"For what?" your child will probably say.

"I've been too laid back in my approach," you could respond, "and I haven't told you the truth. I want to tell you more about life. The reality is that it's a difficult topic to talk about. I've held back, believing that you'll figure all this out on your own, and I've come to the conclusion that it's not your job to figure it out on your own. It's *my* job as your parent to tell you what I believe and why I believe it."

There's your opener to teach your kid whatever you want to tell him or her. Even if your son rolls his eyes and says, "Mom, you told me way too much already. I don't need to know anymore," keep that dialogue open. You're the parent; *you* get to determine what information he needs or doesn't need.

Courage, parents, is not a lack of fear. Courage is acknowledging your fears, facing them head-on, and working through them. Both of us still get nervous talking to our kids—and we teach this stuff professionally! But we follow through nonetheless because we believe it is vitally important for our kids to have the best and most healthy start in life that we can provide.

Don't Ignore Your Own Laundry

As parents, we walk into our marriages, relationships, and family life with a backpack we often don't even realize we're carrying. Inside lies everything that's ever wounded our hearts, minds, and spirits. When we hold the pain in, it surfaces eventually, like a beach ball held underwater.

Once our children enter puberty, they trigger all sorts of memories for us: the guidance we wish we'd had from our parents, the sexual trouble we got into, the things peers and parents said that stuck in our minds, the ridicule we endured because we didn't know as much as our friends. As we guide our kids, their situations will echo our own experiences, memories will emerge vividly, wounds may reopen, and we may react out of what happened to us rather than out of what is best for our children.

Our personal history shapes our priorities and affects how we communicate with our children. Kids walk around with little antennae operating on the frequency of intuition; they're master interpreters of body language and mannerisms and can decode the messages we don't even realize we're sending. In order to guide our kids, we need to deal with our own hurts, or we'll simply pass on our own adolescent angst.

"What is the biggest rock in your backpack?" We have found that that's a good question to ask parents who feel overwhelmed with their problems. Some mothers, for example, whose previous sexual failures make it difficult for them to talk about physical intimacy with their children, seek to compensate by trying to carry their girls through life rather than give them the skills they need to travel on their own.

Listen: this approach doesn't work! Stalling may make it easier for you in the short term, but it's storing up a mess of trouble for both you and your kid in the long run. Since some day you really will have to face your past, it might as well be now, when doing so will benefit your children immensely.

Dr. Leman has written an entire book *(The Real You)* that helps people come to grips with their "rule book," those often unconscious but extremely powerful assumptions about life. If you find issues like this blocking intimacy with your children, you might benefit from unlocking the secrets to your personality by reading this book and carefully considering the impact of your birth order, examining your childhood memories, decoding your love language, and getting a better grip on your personality type.

You may, however, be carrying burdens too heavy to be successfully treated with a book; you may need the professional help of a pastor or counselor. Certain wounds go deep into our childhoods, and it takes time and expertise to deal with them. If you put it off, ultimately your kids will suffer. In essence, they'll have to live with the mess that you refuse to clean up. Taking stock of your own wounds requires courage, but it is important for your health and for the health of your family.

Don't wait! If a red light appears on your car's dashboard, you do something about it right away. You don't wait until your car has broken down in the middle of a desert or on top of a mountain pass. If you sense a deeper issue, that you've been violated in some way, then that's reason enough to make an appointment with a recommended counselor. If nothing comes up in the course of these meetings, move on, knowing you've made contact and that you can return if you need to.

Or maybe you need to discover (or rediscover) the power of being loved by your heavenly Father. We bank on education, status, and power to give us a magic carpet ride out of the sewage we've allowed ourselves to live in, but eventually these feeble attempts reveal themselves as radically insufficient. God is patient, but he's also like the good parent who says to us, "You're going to have to sit still and have your wounds cared for, no matter how much it stings." You can't escape your hurt by putting Band-Aids on something that needs deeper care.

Throughout the Bible, we see characters such as David opening their emotions to God. When I (Kathy) have been working through my sexual development, the highs and the lows, I have put myself in places where I can hear something that will teach me through God's Word and expose me to his grace: Christian counseling, a Bible study group, a radio or television program—something other than the mud I'm already in. We recommend that you begin this journey by reading through the book of Psalms; have you ever felt the emotions that are so vividly described by the psalmists?

Just as your children were not meant to walk this world alone, so you as a parent are not meant to walk this world alone. You have a loving God, eager to guide, comfort, and encourage you.

Putting Puberty Education Back Where It Belongs: The Home

Think about the last time you picked up an apple at the grocery store. Did you say to yourself, "I bet this came from Smith Farms, out in Iowa. It was probably sprayed every six weeks with an insecticide and was picked by a migrant worker named Carlos. They put it in a truck and took it to a warehouse, and from there it was shipped to the store in an 18-wheeler driven by a guy named Mac with a big tattoo on his left arm. Jimmy from produce must have taken it from the back of the store and put the apple right here for me to find it"?

Or have you ever gone past the meat section and said, "Oh, I bet they got those steaks from Old Betsy. Yeah, they fed her just the right grains—and probably injected her with a few steroids—then hauled her away, sliced her up, and wrapped the choicest parts right here for me. Yum-yum"?

We're relatively sure you haven't. Modernization has caused most of us to become disconnected from the source of our food; sadly, modernization has also caused changes in our society that have led many parents to become disconnected from the source of their kids' education.

Your children were designed by God to be raised by a mommy and a daddy. Of the many lifestyle choices touted by today's media, marriage between mommy and daddy still wins out as the best way to raise our kids. Do you want homegrown kids? Then the recipe is quite simple: you'll need to keep your kids around your home. That way you can teach them your values and beliefs as you go about your daily routine, interacting with them and their friends through the normal parts of daily life.

Many parents equate the word *discipline* with punishment, though the word is more closely related to *disciple*—an activity that requires ample time and a shared life to successfully accomplish. Even with such verses as Proverbs 13:24 ("He who spares the rod hates his son"), used by many parents to justify punishment of all sorts, we should "consider how the rod was used in the pastoral culture of Old Testament times. It was an instrument to guide ignorant sheep, not a means of beating them into submission. Note how the verse concludes: '. . . but he who loves him is careful to discipline him.'"[1]

It is through the little things in life that we teach: the way we respond to a spouse's request to wash the dishes, the attention we give our son who wants to show us the multimedia report he's working on for school when we're in the middle of a work project ourselves. The fact is, those of us at home have already been and should continue to be the primary teachers in our child's sexual education. The messages we give our kids will be the ones that form their lives and the decisions they face. If we remain silent, they will get their cues from elsewhere.

Your kids are looking to you for your messages, spoken or unspoken. They can't pick up these messages if they're hanging out at the mall while you're at home. They can't read your reactions if they're always at a friend's house, playing the latest PlayStation game. They can't learn your values if they spend the bulk of their life hanging around their peers.

Why do so many kids insist on becoming overly busy? Because they're desperately searching for intimacy, which is best provided at home! They want a sense of belonging, and if they don't find it with their family, they'll try to create it with their peers. Many kids fall into their peer groups as a last resort. They tried to reach out to their parents but met only resounding silence.

One thirteen-year-old girl told *O* magazine, "I wish my mom didn't go nuts every time I mention the word *sex.*"

That mom, unfortunately, is missing out on the opportunity to be the primary teacher for her daughter regarding her sexuality. What her daughter craves, the magazine points out, "is an unflappable parent who makes herself approachable about any topic.... What girls really long for is the same closeness, the same eyeball-to-eyeball connection with family, the same lingering embrace after a long day that I want.... When they don't get it from those who love them, they seek it from strangers who can't give it to them."

We all need intimacy, especially a child experiencing massive life changes who's also looking for a social—a *familial*—context in which he or she fits. Speaking of the sex she had with at least fifteen partners, another girl in the article explained the rationale for her explicit behavior: "I just wanted to feel better, to feel close to someone."[2]

Intimacy really is at the heart of this book. Our kids search for intimacy as they become increasingly aware of the opposite sex, and we provide intimacy by loving them, listening to them, and guiding them down a path they have never trod—a path you know firsthand, whether it was an easy one for you or not. For many pubescent girls who become sexually active, sexuality isn't so much about "having sex" as it is about fitting in or feeling close to someone—a need so strong that they will violate the dictates of their own consciences to get it. If they don't feel close to you, Mom and Dad, or if they don't have a sense of fitting into the family, they'll seek other relationships to try to fulfill that desire.

Many of you picked up this book hoping to straighten out your kid. That's an understandable quest. But before you go on, we hope you'll seriously consider the challenges in this chapter to address your own issues! That's where sexual education starts—in the home, with a healthy parent.

Chapter 3

"He's Doing What Daddy Taught Him to Do"

Creating a Home Environment That Will Grow Sexually Healthy Kids

Seven-year-old Deion Sanders, son of the former All-Pro NFL super-star who shares the same name, got flagged after scoring a touchdown in a youth football game. Apparently, young Sanders went a little overboard doing a dance in the end zone after making such a big play. The little tyke kept writhing around until the referee blew his whistle and threw a yellow flag, signaling a penalty.

Deion's dad—one of the flashiest players to ever suit up for a football contest—complained, "Why you gotta throw a flag? He's doing what Daddy taught him to do."[1]

Our kids are watching, learning, and (even more terrifying) copying our behavior! In light of this, how does a parent lay the foundation of a good example? How does a father or mother create a strong enough relationship with Susie Q that she will approach them openly with her questions about sex?

Such a track record gets built over time.

Character growth doesn't happen overnight, or in a week, or a month, or even a year. It happens slowly, like the measured, ring-by-ring growth of a redwood tree. It takes time and discipline to make significant, positive change and often involves sacrifice. As his child grows, a dad takes a cut in pay to spend more time with his toddler, years later disciplines his kindergartener even though his parents never disciplined him, and when the time comes, gathers courage to answer his pubescent's questions about sex (which his father never discussed). Not one of these steps was easy, but his decisions set him on a new course, and step by step he traveled what Eugene Peterson calls a "long obedience in the same direction."

You're already establishing a track record with your kid by how you listen, by what you say when you get angry, and by how you treat your spouse. We like to surprise parents with our answer to the question, "When do I start talking about sex?"

The answer is, you've already started.

Sex Ed Begins on the Changing Table

"I've got PMS, so leave me alone!" a mother yells at her kids as they get ready for school. She turns to her daughter as they grab their coats. "You better get used to it, honey, because your time is coming!"

As she passes her son on the front steps, she mumbles, "And you'll have a wife someday, so you better learn to live with it, too!"

Sex ed goes way back, even to the time when you began potty-training your daughter. Back to how you handled your three-year-old son's runny nose. Back to what you said to your five-year-old daughter when she had her hand in her pants in the grocery-store parking lot. Through all the things you've said about bodily functions—spitting, runny noses, bowel movements, passing gas, your own period—you've been teaching them how to think about their bodies. They've been watching you; even more than that, they've been *studying* you, trying to learn what they can.

Dads, you're instructing your kids in sex ed by how you look at women and by how you treat your wife. Moms, you communicate volumes by how you treat your husband. If you've essentially been teaching your daughter to view her body as a sexual receptacle, she's in big trouble when Billy comes along ready to use her as one.

The worst approach toward sex ed is to create seemingly catchy one-liners that don't get reinforced. Even the cleverest of sayings rarely stick if not backed up with authentic example. *How you live your life* is the most powerful sex ed lesson your child will ever receive.

Consider NBA All-Star Jason Kidd. As a basketball player, Jason finds and creates passing lanes that few could imagine, which makes him a fan favorite as well as a welcomed teammate for those who benefit from his passes.

But his story has its dark side.

After five years of marriage, tension in the Kidd household had become pretty thick. On January 18, 2001, the pressure exploded when Joumana (Jason's wife) told Jason not to pick at T. J.'s (their son's) food. Jason responded by spitting a french fry at her. Then he punched her in the face.

T. J. was watching, and learning.

Joumana fled upstairs and locked herself in the bathroom. She called 911, then hung up. Following protocol, the 911 dispatchers called back, and Jason answered the phone. He handed it to Joumana, who told the dispatcher what had happened. A while later, T. J. was still watching as the police took his dad away.

To his credit, Jason has worked hard at controlling his rage. He's been faithful in counseling. He told Joumana that calling the police was the right thing to do. Jason's therapist says she has worked with athletes on about two hundred cases of violence, and not a single one has responded "as positively" as Jason has.

But the damage had already been done.

Sports Illustrated reporter S. L. Price observed how T. J. already imitates Jason's dribble and his foul-line stance "with astonishing accuracy." Unfortunately, that's not all T. J. imitates.

Price watched as Jason filmed a commercial—a long, arduous, and usually boring task. T. J. was running out of patience. Joumana did her best to keep T. J. from getting in the way, which would only delay the shoot and make them have to start all over again.

In a desperate attempt to distract her son, Joumana grabbed hold of him and asked, "Did you have a nice time at school?"

According to the reporter, T. J. turned and hit her "square in the cheek" with his right hand. Joumana simply grabbed his hand and repeated her question.

T. J. hit her again and then walked away. Instead of disciplining her son, Joumana rolled a ball his way; T. J. laughed, picked it up, and started dribbling it, just like his dad.[2]

All of Jason's remorse couldn't remove that indelible mark he made when he set an example for his son by hitting his wife. Unfortunately, Joumana is also setting an example by allowing her son to hit her. Sadly, little T. J. received an unfortunate instruction in sex ed just by coming to the dinner table.

They write magazine articles about Jason's violent act. Most of us live in homes where sick patterns of relating take place. But because we're not famous, the police don't get called and our failings get no press, *but they do get passed on*. If you finish this section thinking only about how all athletes are no-good bums who take advantage of others, you've completely missed the point.

We're appalled that a man would hit his wife in the face, and we're saddened that a mom would let her son repeat the action without setting consequences; but if a reporter were to come into *your* house, what unhealthy patterns would he uncover? What sad teaching would he be able to recount?

When you have kids, you teach by example. The example may be a positive one, a negative one, or more likely, a mixture of the two. But you're always teaching. That's why, in the previous chapter, we stressed dealing with your own negative issues, lest those same issues get passed down to your children.

But while setting an example is important, there also comes a time when we must use words. How's your information highway?

How's Your Highway?

Imagine a country road that winds through rolling hills, takes you over a covered bridge, and then leads you up and down switchbacks from which you can see the valley for miles. Sadly, you haven't traveled this road for years, and neither has anyone else. It's run-down, overgrown with weeds pushing up through the cracks, and peppered with potholes. The centerlines look so faded by weather that you can no longer tell where the lanes are. Some of the guardrails have washed down the hillside where the land eroded during heavy rains.

Now imagine you have to drive that stretch of road during a stormy winter's night. The ice makes those curves high above the valley very treacherous. The bridge may even have washed out—hard to tell. But you have to drive this stretch of road because a loved one at the other end—a friend, a relative, your son or daughter—needs you.

Too often this word picture most closely resembles the reality when parents approach one of us about talking to their children. They have let the highway of their communication with their children break down, and now something has happened that makes them more than a little nervous; they find condoms in their son's sock drawer, they hear whispers, their daughter's attire shocks them, and they panic. Now that they need to get through to their kids, they want to know how to traverse that treacherous but long-neglected stretch of highway called parent-child communication.

Sadly, many parents leave this road entirely untended until a crisis hits. If you put off highway maintenance and let the road fall into disrepair, though you may make every effort to travel that road during a crisis, if your child doesn't feel comfortable with the road, he or she won't meet you on it. *Why should I turn to you now?* your child may think. *I've gotten along all by myself up to this point.*

Parents with a good, well-maintained highway of communication are going to feel much more secure when the unknown comes. Why? They've paved the way by first talking through very simple things with their kids.

Both of us have seen that the greatest foundation you can give to a child for positive sexual education is an involved and caring parent. Unfortunately, we live in the e-mail age, in which the thinking goes, *The less said, the better*. E-mail is great for project management at the office but lousy for communication at home. Sure, it's quick and convenient, but "BTW, :–6. GtG. TTYL; NRN [[Lauren]]" doesn't foster an intimate relationship with a young daughter. (For the uninitiated, that's "By the way, [I'm] exhausted. Got to go. Talk to you later; no reply necessary. Hugs to Lauren.") Is that the way your family communicates, e-mailing each other all day?

Or maybe you're the kind of family that phones each other, talking absentmindedly as you walk from room to room, focused on your own business, more interested in checking off tasks in your daily planner than in how your blood relatives are faring in this journey called life. Which is more important to you—how clean your kid's room is or the reason why your kid is so distraught he can't bring himself to clean it at the moment?

Without doubt, the life of a parent sometimes feels like that of a CEO, CFO, janitor, chauffeur, and COO *combined*. There are bills to pay, rides to give, house chores to be monitored—feeding the dog, taking out the garbage, and recycling on Monday morning—and the list runs on. But when you replay the day's tape, do you truly *connect* in your interactions with your kids? What exactly are you running, a home or a hotel business? A hotel is based on temporary stays and business relationships; a home is based on long-term relationships and mutual empowerment. If you live as if you're running a hotel, too interested in your own affairs to wait in the school auditorium for your kid's only line in the school play, your message when it comes to teaching your child to wait until marriage for sex will still be "DWISNWID" ("Do what I say, not what I do").

Making Time for Your Masterpiece

Face it: raising a child isn't an efficient business! The energy you expend in raising one child is like that of an artist pouring years into a single work. Michelangelo spent three years creating his sculpture *David*, and it took him more than four years to paint the ceiling of the Sistine Chapel. Raising a kid takes roughly *eighteen* years. Creating a masterpiece takes time—lots of it.

Slow down. Kids require attention, and with all the changes going on during puberty, you're going to have to make time and space for them. You can't switch to autopilot as a parent just because your son can now fix himself a sandwich or give the dog water. Parenting at this stage isn't something you can whip through, and why would you want to?

Before we talk about disciplines to teach your children, let's talk about a few disciplines that you can apply yourself:

Don't pack your calendar. Take a look at your calendar. Is it packed with church committees, PTA meetings, volunteer commitments at the local shelter, choir practice, and small group leadership? Get rid of anything that takes you away from the time you need to be with your family. These may be excellent activities, but if they're taking time away from a family who needs you, you're doing both them and yourself a disservice. The years of your child's puberty are critical; once your kids reach a certain age, you're done.

It's not enough to reserve time for the urgent; family intimacy gets built around "nonessential" time like tossing a ball around, making a mess of the kitchen while baking cookies, going out for pizza together, spontaneously talking about whatever comes up on the spur of the moment and really listening and getting involved in what your kids are doing. You have to leave mental space to direct them; you can't effectively parent while fully wrapped up in your work.

Open or closed? As a parent, you wear a sign that says either Open or Closed. This refers to not only how open or closed you are to your kid's questions but also the transparency with which you help your child work through issues facing him or her.

Your daughter, for example, may feel insecure about her body changes. Perhaps toward the beginning of puberty she feels her body is growing disproportionately, something you are thinking about your body, as well. On a mother-daughter shopping trip, you may admit to the saleswoman, "My hips are big. I need to focus on a center point. I know there are ladies larger than me wearing pants that look great." When your daughter hears you talking openly about your strengths and weaknesses, she learns to accept her own body quirks. Pay attention to your child's issues and model behavior through your own life. Your kids will feel more open to asking questions, including those about sex later on, when they hear you talking about the very things they're dealing with.

Taking your kids on dates. You felt special the last time someone took you out, didn't you? The same is true for your kids when you spend time with them. They've seen you focus on work, on church events, on your spouse, and when you make your children the center of attention for an afternoon, an evening, or even an occasional weekend, it sends their esteem through the roof. Adults still remember childhood outings with their parents: movies, dinners, hikes, shopping trips, ball games. Those outings become highlights of a kid's month. Your son may always remember the simple thrill of having a hot dog at the stadium, "one of the guys" with his dad.

I (Kathy) often took my son John out on dates after school. Even though I'm a woman, I learned how to speak his language: we got something to eat! Those dates gave us a chance to talk about school, sports, and at times, issues coming up in his life. When John was listening in that public restaurant or mall food court, he remained on his best behavior. Our dates empowered me to comment on what I saw in him so that we could work on it together. One-on-one time also gives kids permission to voice their honest reactions in a relaxed environment.

Evening and morning: precious times. When John and Amy were in their puberty years, I (Kathy) found that they best unloaded the day during the evening hour just before bed; that's when I could parent most effectively. I would give a half hour to each child as they got ready and then lay in bed, and they would tell me crucial things that had happened to them that day. Don't neglect this time. Just before bed, kids become open to being parented in ways that they sometimes aren't during the rest of the day. Your kids are more vulnerable during this time, and the conversations held during these evening and morning times can provide healing bookends to a day that may have been difficult or confusing or scary—or fun!

Simplify. Throwing your son or daughter onto a soccer team does not necessarily make them better kids; activities are not intrinsically good. One of the saddest commentaries on our society today is that we actually use children's activities to define our own identities. Soccer moms, for example. While some activities can be worthwhile in moderation, overdosing on them dilutes the bond between parent and child. Doing *too* much shifts the focus of the family to the kids, rather than where it should be—on the parents. Keep activities to a healthy minimum. Dr. Leman recommends one activity per child per term. Some will argue against this, but kids should never become the centerpieces of the family; that place belongs to the husband and wife.

Hannah, Dr. Leman's fifteen-year-old daughter, had to choose between volleyball and drama. She ultimately decided to take part in the play *Bye-Bye Birdie*. Next semester she'll be on the basketball team. Lauren, Dr. Leman's youngest daughter, is in Girl Scouts, which meets twice a month after school plus an occasional field trip or Saturday hike. That's enough.

Why is limiting activities so important? A busy parent will miss a child's most subtle—and often most important—signals. We have to slow down enough that we can listen to their hearts, not their words.

Listen to Their Hearts, Not Their Words

It was an ultimatum delivered with all the passion of a young woman in true distress: "Under no circumstances will you come to my first volleyball game," Krissy Leman told her parents.

Krissy had reached that point in a kid's life when part of her didn't even want to admit she *had* a parent. She said her mother yelled too loudly, and she didn't want a parent trailing her, screaming like a banshee, at a game ninety miles from home.

Now, deep down, did Krissy really want her parents to come? Yes. While Sande, her mother, didn't end up going, I drove to see it, and Krissy admitted she was happy that I came.

Parents, you need to understand that no matter what kids say, they really do want you to stay involved in their lives, in appropriate ways that don't embarrass them. They want your approval and affirmation. They want your attention and even your guidance.

Since they are still kids, they may not verbalize this desire; they may even say the opposite. But *you* need to be an adult about this, recognizing that their feelings are a maelstrom right now. You ultimately know what is best for them. You need to admit, *Hey, I am the parent here. I am going to come alongside my son or daughter. I am not going to run her over, but I'm going to be involved in her life.*

Unfortunately, many parents get too busy with their own rat race to take time for their kids. Trust and bonding takes time; it isn't instant Jell-O. If you refuse to take the time to know your kids well enough to decipher what they really mean when you ask, "Would you like to rehearse your lines with me for the school play?" and they say, "I don't care," when they really, *really* do care, then you'll both miss out.

Because it's often more difficult for fathers to read between the lines with their daughters and for mothers to intuitively understand their sons, sex ed often gets limited to talks "woman to woman" and "man to man." We think healthy sex education needs to be just the opposite.

Sons Need Moms; Daughters Need Dads

Scientists have been combing this earth for decades now, and the news is in: they still have not found a wife who loves to be grabbed by her husband. Held, yes. Cuddled, stroked softly—you bet. Yet in the Leman counseling room, I find such a thought to be revolutionary for men! They express shock. They think all that pinching, grabbing, and poking is a turn-on! Many of them would love it if their wives grabbed at them, so they can't understand why the reverse isn't also true.

Males and females are very different, and who better to deliver this message to a son than his mother? Who better than a father to give accurate information about boys to a girl?

To be honest, a good bit of my (Dr. Leman's) counseling practice involves undoing the bad advice given to brides by their mothers and to sons by their fathers. Because we have this mistaken notion that sex ed is best done on a same-sex basis, sometimes hilarious myths get passed down from one generation to the next.

Let's be honest: men are better equipped to tell a daughter why a twelve-year-old boy would push her to do something sexually, because they've been twelve-year-old boys! Dads, talk to your daughters about how men view women. Moms, talk to your sons about how women view men and how women want to be treated.

During early pubescence, when Dad affirms his young daughter, he's really affirming her femininity. Girls and boys grow into their own person during puberty and begin wanting more and more the attention of the other gender. Who better to fill that growing need than the people who were there at the beginning?

Ten-year-old Lauren Leman often waits up for me when I come home from trips and wakes up to say good-bye when I leave early in the morning. In fact, I *have* to wake her up to say good-bye and give her a hug and a kiss when I travel. If I don't—even on those mornings I leave at 4:30 A.M. to catch an early flight—my wife hears about it the whole week.

One night while waiting up for me, Lauren fell asleep on the couch, wearing a purple wig she was thinking of using for part of her Halloween costume. When I arrived in the morning, I went over to her and rubbed her back. "Here's Mommy to wake you up," I feigned in a high, squeaky voice. When Lauren realized it was me, she instantly awoke and flew into my arms, obviously thrilled and delighted to be with her dad again.

That father-daughter, mother-son connection (Dr. Leman addresses the former in his book *What a Difference a Daddy Makes*) is critical during these years. If ever there is a time for cross-gender parent-child connection, it's this time—puberty—ages eight through fourteen, the developmental years heading into adolescence.

A strong, intimate connection between the opposite-sex parent and the pubescent child lays the groundwork for a confident, self-directed adolescent.

Charting a Course into Adolescence: Self-Directed Kids

"What are you doing about John's curfew?" a mother asked Kathy Bell.

"What do you mean?" Kathy replied.

"I'm arguing with my son because his friend is staying out until between one and three in the morning and he wants to do the same. I don't want to allow that."

"Well, don't," Kathy replied.

"But how do you talk about that?"

Curfew had become a huge issue for this mother and her son, with violent arguments breaking out over it. Kathy's answer to the mother's question didn't really matter much, because it wasn't what Kathy said to her son in setting the family rule that actually made the difference. What made the difference? The track record Kathy and her son had developed over the years.

By the time the Bell children had turned fourteen, fifteen, and sixteen—moving out of puberty into adolescence—Kathy and her children had already reached a high level of trust and open communication. They knew each other's track records. Most of their patterns had been set by eighth grade, and as her children entered high school, Kathy began to let go of the reins more and more, weighing pros and cons with them and letting them make decisions, even though Kathy and her husband reserved the right to make the final call.

Guess what happened? By high school, John was making decisions *on his own.* He chose to opt out of football for other sports, for example, to avoid the players' intense pressure to party and drink. He chose not to play football through his senior year, even though he loved football, was one of the most popular guys in the school, and would have been playing for a team that was a former state champion.

Sadly, many parents do the opposite. They get so busy during their kid's pubescence that they pull back, but then when they notice scary behavior in their kid during adolescence, they suddenly and frantically try to rein him back in. This is the reverse of a healthy pattern of parenting. You should be more involved when they're younger and then gradually allow them to become more self-directed.

Let your kids in on what you're doing! Consider a conversation that has had great success in the Leman household.

"The neat thing about this thing called life is that Dad and Mom don't walk around with you for the rest of it. We don't monitor what you say and what you do every moment of the day. There's no way we could do that even if we wanted to. But we have great belief that you can handle the things that come your way.

"There's going to come a day when you may think Dad and Mom are the two most out-of-it people in the world (if that day hasn't already come!). But here are some things we think are going to happen to you: you'll see and hear things that are not appropriate, that are filthy, and that are disrespectful. Kids are going to say things to you like, 'Drink this, smoke this, snort this—it's fun.' In those moments, honey, it's up to you how you are going to respond. It's your life, not mine or your Mom's, not your brother's or your sister's. We want you to know that we believe in you. Like a lot of things in life, there are times you'll need help, and I hope we can talk as we've always talked."

We want all our children to become responsible, self-directed adults. That's why the Leman kids write the checks for the house bills when they're eleven or twelve, which not only teaches them the value of money but also helps them give back to the family and fosters belonging. They know how important those bills are, and giving them that responsibility gives them an added sense of importance and belonging. In the end, you're giving your kids the skills to live life, whether the skill is balancing the home budget or saying no when pressured to have sex before marriage.

Becoming self-directed will help your children as they enter the many embarrassing moments that accompany pubescence. The day rapidly approaches when they will need and appreciate increased privacy.

If He Can Rebuild the Computer, He Can Operate the Dryer

"How many of you can run a microwave?" Kathy asked the boys in her father-son class.

"I can!" the boys all replied enthusiastically.

"How many of you can run the DVD player?"

"Me! Me!" they answered.

"How many of you can run the computer?"

"I know how to do that!"

Then Kathy threw the curve. "Well, then you can wash your own sheets."

"No way!" they protested.

"Let me tell you why you would want to do this," Kathy added. "Because one day in the not-too-distant future, you're going to wake up in the middle of the night from your first wet dream. How many of you want to tell your mom the next morning that you had a wet dream, and would she please wash your sheets? Okay, I can see most of you would be too embarrassed to do that. What's your other option? You could do nothing, but how many of you want to climb back into crusty sheets the next night?"

Kathy gives young girls similar advice. "You're going to start your period, and you're going to get blood on the bed. No matter how careful you are, sooner or later it's going to happen. Who wants to explain to their mother or father—or worse yet, their older brother—why you need your sheets or underwear washed in cold water? If you have already built a track record by washing your own sheets before the need arrives, when you wake up having made a slight mess, nobody is going to look at you funny as you walk down the hallway with your sheets in the morning. Nobody will ask, 'What are you doing?'"

Parents, if your kid can run the microwave, configure the PPP on your computer's dial-up account, and program the VCR weeks in advance, then surely he can operate the washer and dryer. If you'll just take the time to train your child in a few simple skills, you'll build a track record together, you can begin holding him or her accountable, and you'll build in your child the sense of responsibility that is so essential as a young person matures into adolescence.

The Power of Positive Expectations

If it's a school night at the Leman house, there are four words you won't hear from my mouth: "Do you have homework?" Our kids know if they have homework, and they don't need me to remind them of it.

"But, Dr. Leman!" some parents protest, "What's wrong with a little reminder?"

If you talk to your children, you'll find that reminders aren't called "reminders." They're called "nagging." But expectations develop responsibility. I want my kids to become self-directed.

Of course, it's not as if we fail to pay attention. In our kids' school system, we receive interim reports, and if one of our kids is falling down a bit in, say, math or English, we'll find out about it in the report. Perhaps we'll need to schedule time with a teacher to do some extra work. Our daughter, Lauren, stayed after school for a while, and she soon got back on top of it. But never did we hover over her like hummingbirds, constantly buzzing in her ear about what she needed to do. Instead, we lifted her up with positive expectation.

I can't underscore positive expectation enough. For while I'm concerned about my daughter's math, I'm *passionately* concerned that she make wise decisions about her body. Teaching her how to be responsible with homework will ultimately teach her how to handle sexually related issues, as well. Our kids have to learn how to be self-directed and how to detect those warning signs that God gives to us.

We like to teach kids what we call the "Uh-oh Phenomenon." When you're in social situations and you feel that little *uh-oh* inside—you know something's wrong. It's that Jiminy Cricket–like voice from our shoulder, our conscience, telling us that all might not be well in the world. That's the time to get out. That's the time to leave. That's the time to turn away. That's the time to stop what you're doing and say to your boyfriend or girlfriend, "Hey, let's go in a different direction." In other words, the decisions a young woman makes while in the back seat of a car when she's sixteen or seventeen are often forged by nonsexually related decisions she made when she was eight or nine.

Sara is a good case in point. She had been selling magazine sub-scriptions house to house—taking people's orders, collecting money, and earning a commission on her sales. The problem was that Sara kept the money and never turned in the orders. Sad as that may seem, what is even more sad is that she never turned them in simply because she wasn't good at following through; she hadn't developed that skill. By fifth grade, Sara was stealing money from her mother's purse, and by seventh grade, she was shoplifting. In eighth grade, she finally got caught shoplifting in the mall.

Many adults might point a finger at peer pressure, but when Kathy talked with Sara, she discovered an entirely different perspective. Sara said she started stealing money from her mother's purse not because her friends pressured her to do so but simply because she wanted money to buy ice cream and pencils at the school store back when she was in fifth grade. She was even willing to work hard to get what she wanted, which was why she began selling the magazines in the first place. If someone had been there to help her develop responsible money-handling skills, she would have had money and most likely never gotten into trouble.

For many pubescent kids, getting into trouble is not about peer pres-sure; it's about an intense desire, a drive to do something, a motivation to move to a higher level, and not having someone to teach them the skills they need to achieve these things in a healthy way. Our young people are often left groping around, trying to find their way and place in the world. And sometimes they inadvertently find trouble where they had mostly good intentions.

Clearly, building a track record with your kid helps spell success. I (Kathy) can walk into a classroom of fifth graders and know whether a parent has missed passing on an essential social skill. When I see Joe Cool continuing to talk during study time, I know that he needs a boundary, whereas Susie Q can be left alone. I can tell a lot about each student's relationship with their parents when they can't move past the fun and games or when they feel the need to continue joking about something we're talking about. For instance, if I'm talking about breast buds, I'll ask the boys if they realize that they will have breast buds, too. A boy might shoot up his hand to share that that had happened to him. "Really?" the others say, and the class erupts in discussion. But when we try to move on and a certain handful of kids keeps giggling, cracking jokes, and making crude comments as they seek to draw more attention to themselves, I know they haven't been set up well for success. More than likely, such kids never had boundaries enforced at home.

Certain skills should be in place by fifth grade to help your kid achieve social success: knowing the routine, learning to wait, following through, developing foresight, managing time, gaining mastery over feelings, and respecting authority. If these external structures are not solidly in place by fifth grade, then when hormones turn kids' internal structures into a maelstrom, it can lead to chaos despite your attempts to hold them responsible to observe boundaries they never learned. Without these skills, your children risk getting involved in harmful or antisocial behavior.

Knowing the routine. In the Bell household, we have worked hard to develop basic routines and patterns. One night one of my daughters didn't seem to be getting it.

"Elizabeth," I said to my then seven-year-old daughter, "it's time to get ready for bed. You need to put your stuff away."

"Okay," she said, though a few minutes later she was still coloring.

"Elizabeth, did you not hear me?"

Is this direct defiance? I wondered. *What is Lizzie thinking about so intensely that she's continuing to disregard my directions?* I walked up to her, made eye contact, and put my hand on her shoulder to help bring her back to the routine at hand.

Your child's faithfulness in getting ready in the morning, meeting you after school at the designated spot for pick up, going to bed, and getting chores done are all signs that your kid understands the process, order, and flow of your family's routine. How many times will a kid get into trouble because of a lack of order to your home, because the routine continually changes, or because you send confusing messages regarding expectations? Creating a stable, secure home life cultivates trust between you and your child—a crucial thing when it comes to sharing vulnerably about sexuality.

If I hadn't followed up with Elizabeth, I would have cooperated with chaos. Then Elizabeth would have started thinking, *Well, maybe I don't really have to go to bed at a certain time or put away my things at night.* I reminded her of the routine, and she yielded with little pressure because that's the way things have always been: clear expectations, clear responsibilities, and assumed obedience.

When a kid grows up with eighteen years of solid routine—Dad (and possibly Mom) going to work, chores getting done, the family eating dinners together, work and play being done on the weekends, and so on—he learns that life has a certain order. When you begin talking to this boy about how marriage comes before sex, he already has an innate understanding and appreciation for doing things the right way.

Having said this, we also have to recognize that today's world can be a very, very busy place in which to raise children. An element of chaos exists by the sheer factor of time required to do even one activity; just one child's sport can mean driving across a city, occasionally putting off dinner, and juggling diverse schedules.

That's okay; while we want to strive for the ideal—a nice, peaceful home, with everything done in order and with no interruptions—we have to admit that real life contains its share of chaos. You need to give yourself permission to just slow it down, mentally, no matter where you are. Your devotional quiet time, for instance, may be behind the wheel of the car. Your kitchen-table sex ed may be done while you're walking through the grocery store or driving through the drive-up window at a fast-food restaurant. It's just as important to learn how to be at peace in chaos as it is to establish a solid routine.

Though it may sound like we're talking out of both sides of our mouths—establish a routine, become comfortable with chaos—the truth is our children need both skills! When we talk with them about the body, we're asking kids to look for order: they are kids, their bodies mature, they become adults, they get married, they become sexually active, they have kids, and so on. When they live in a world of external order, internal order makes more sense.

But any order gets challenged at times. Though they *know* the correct order is to delay sex until marriage, their body may be screaming for sexual activity *now*. How they see you maintain peace and equilibrium in chaos will speak volumes to them about how peaceful they can be in spite of the chaos going on in their bodies.

One thing that worked well in the Bell household has been to respond to pressure or chaos with a familiar hum (Ho-hummm). Whenever one of us does that, it signals that we're in a quandary and are pausing to figure out what to say or do. The other family members back off to give that person some space. This has been a very valuable skill for our children to learn, for while we strive to present as much order as possible, we have to recognize that our kids will occasionally face chaos.

Learning to wait. A week before Kathy and her kids were to take a commercial flight, she bought each of them a gift, which she wrapped and set in plain sight on the counter. They knew the rule: "You can look at your box, you can pick it up, but you may not open it. It must stay there until our trip, and then on the plane you can open it." The kids had a hard time restraining themselves, but Kathy explained that she was helping them learn to wait (what we call delayed gratification).

"I know you *really* want this," Kathy sympathized with her children, "and the time will come in a few days when you can have it. But for now you must wait." Her words had to be enough for them in the meantime, something on which they could focus their hopes. Kathy knew that one day—sooner rather than later—she would not be able to control her kids' behavior, including their sexual behavior, so she wanted to teach them how to wait for something they wanted very much.

If you always give in to your children's demands, if no pleasure is ever put off, they'll enter adolescence with no learned ability to delay gratification. And in our society of untold temptations, who wants any of our children to lack the ability to delay gratification?

Following through. Does your child understand the consequences of not following through? Dr. Leman teaches what has come to be known as "reality discipline" (see his book *Making Children Mind without Losing Yours*). Reality discipline means you don't nag, you don't beg, you don't yell. You simply allow your children to face the consequences of their irresponsibility. If the chores don't get done, they miss that party, that game, or that favorite television show. In other words, they pay the price and learn valuable lessons when their parents let them face the consequences of irresponsible behavior.

This is far more beneficial in building self-directed kids than screaming out threats, giving time-outs, or even grounding them. If we don't finish a book on time or show up when one of us has been invited to speak, we don't get paid and our families may not be able to pay the mortgage. As adults, we have had to learn how to follow through on our commitments, even when it is painful (like the time Dr. Leman had unbelievably good seats to the NCAA Final Four basketball tournament but had to let them go due to a previously agreed upon speaking engagement). Kids need this same skill; the more closely their lives echo real life—with consequences and the like—the better prepared they'll be.

Developing foresight. No one can succeed in today's world without the crucial skill of foresight. Our children must be taught to slow down and consider the most likely consequences of their actions. This obviously has all sorts of ramifications when it comes to sexuality and the choices they will make in their relationships.

We like to remind parents of the benefit of using surprise. Let's say your daughter has a birthday party to go to at one o'clock on Saturday afternoon. She knows that every Saturday her room has to be cleaned and the dog flops need to be cleaned up from the back yard. A reality-discipline parent won't nag her about this; they may not even remind her. She knows what needs to be done and expectations get set accordingly.

Which means that if she has spent all morning watching television or reading teen novels and doesn't get her work done, and then she comes to you at 12:45 P.M., saying, "I'm ready to go, Daddy," then you'll say, "Oh, but I can't take you. Your room isn't cleaned. The back yard still has dog flops all over it."

Letting her get all dressed up and ready for the party increases the benefit of this tremendous disappointment. Her shock at suddenly not being able to go will teach her that by avoiding foresight, she lost out on a cherished activity. She needed to look ahead and think, *If I want to be ready to have fun by one o'clock, I better get my work done in the morning.*

You usually have to do this only once or twice before your kids catch on and become *very* foresighted!

Parents, don't be soft on this! If your kids don't learn foresight, they'll grab immediate sexual gratification, chase after the thrill of drugs, and throw themselves headlong into the rush of dangerous behavior (driving too fast, taking stupid risks, and the like) without looking ahead and considering the consequences of their actions. You've got to let them learn to face the sting of stupid choices. Failure and its corresponding consequences are best tasted as an eight-year-old who misses a birthday party, rather than as a seventeen-year-old who is paralyzed because he was driving while drunk, or as a sixteen-year-old who gets pregnant on prom night.

Managing time. By fifth grade, kids have to know that "the clock is the boss." As parents, we often make this skill difficult for our kids because we ourselves model poor behavior. How many times do we tell kids, "It's time to go," but then keep talking for another fifteen minutes?

How frequently do you mismanage your own schedule and come whipping into the school parking lot to drop your child off at the last minute (maybe even driving erratically and unsafely on the way)?

Once again, scolding and nagging never taught a kid anything. Letting her face the consequences will.

Take this example. You say, "Dinner is ready!" and one child insists on finishing a computer game. Fifteen minutes later, he rambles into the kitchen and sits down. What did he learn? Disrespect. Tardiness. Taking you for granted.

Now imagine if he walked into the kitchen, saw everyone eating, and noticed that his plate was missing!

"Where's my plate?"

"You weren't here, so we figured you weren't hungry."

"That's crazy!" he'll say, reaching for the cupboard.

"Sorry, Bobby, but there's no dinner for you tonight. Next time, come when we call you."

You'll have to do this only once until he learns that when you say dinner is ready, you mean dinner is ready *now*, not in fifteen minutes.

Teaching our children to respect time is one small way of helping them to cultivate inner responsibility.

Gaining mastery over feelings. If you attended a Kathy Bell sex-ed presentation at a public school, you'd hear her say time and time again, "Don't wait for desire to do the right thing." That's Kathy's way of saying that kids need to learn to set aside how they feel about something in order to rationally choose what's best.

If women who suffered because of absent or abusive fathers follow their feelings, they will choose the wrong man nine and a half times out of ten. We're not saying you should deny or suppress your feelings, but all of us need to learn to examine our feelings and then act out of wisdom rather than emotion.

This begins earlier than you'd expect. For example, you teach a five-year-old how to handle fear by walking her through her emotions and not letting those emotions run over her. "This dog won't hurt you, Amy; go ahead and pet it."

You teach a toddler how to be angry without resorting to violence. "Of course you were upset, Michael, but you know that hitting another child isn't an appropriate response. What else could you have done?"

In the same way, we need to teach our pubescent children that feeling "in love" shouldn't lower their standards for the type of people they hang around with. If a person abuses drugs or acts cruelly toward others, he's not a good choice for a boyfriend, no matter how you feel when you're with him. We also need to teach our children that feelings shouldn't lead them to ignore past friendships. A common failing for young kids just discovering the opposite sex is to become so infatuated with someone that they break off all their old friendships, wanting to spend every moment with their new boyfriend or girlfriend. This is another case where feelings run amok.

If kids can learn to handle feelings early on, they'll be well prepared to stand firm when their feelings run wild at a party and their boyfriend or girlfriend tries to coax them into a back room.

Respecting authority. Though your pubescent kid may feel he's in charge, we've got news for him: he's not. He's not even close to being in charge! There are so many authorities over him that it's not even funny: teachers, principals, coaches, his skin, his hair—and not least, you, his parent. A healthy submission to authority is important at this stage in his development.

Teaching your child to submit to these authorities has great spiritual value because ultimately you want your son or daughter to submit to their heavenly Father. We've talked about raising "self-directed" kids, but what if their self-compass points in the wrong direction? That's where God and a properly formed conscience come into play. Even more important than being self-directed is submitting to God and to the beliefs by which you live your life.

God is there when you can't be. He's present when that cigarette is being passed around behind the gym. God remains nearby when your daughter's boyfriend tries to stick his hand inside her shirt. God is watching when your son gets challenged to steal that six-pack of beer.

A kid who hasn't learned to respect his parents or his teachers probably won't respect God. And a kid with no respect for God can get him or herself into a lot of trouble these days.

As your child develops these life skills—accepting routine, learning how to wait, following through on responsibilities, developing foresight, managing time, mastering their emotions, and submitting to authority—she will be in a much better position to deal with the drive she feels to begin making a place for herself in the world. Your son or daughter will also become much better prepared to confront the lure of peer pressure, to which we'll now turn our attention.

Chapter 4

Peer-Pressure Panic

Understanding and Confronting the Roots of Peer Pressure

Justin Kreutzmann, the son of Grateful Dead drummer Bill Kreutzmann, was still in his first decade of life when his dad said, "Go in the bathroom." The Grateful Dead was scheduled to perform on *Saturday Night Live,* and NBC wanted urine samples before the group—infamous for its drug use—was allowed on air.

Justin saw six little cups, all lined up, and instinctively knew that he was supposed to fill them with his own urine.

"Get me some water!" the little boy pleaded.[1]

Justin didn't complain too much. After all, not many kids can start the day by ordering three cartons of ice cream from room service, and end it with a roomful of female groupies closer in age to him than to his dad.

Being the child of a rock star certainly presents some unique challenges. Francesa Gregorini, Ringo Starr's stepdaughter, said, "It was opulence and beauty and sickness and despair. All swirling."[2]

Having a famous dad doesn't necessarily mean you're proud of him, of course. Kimberly Stewart tried—unsuccessfully, as it turns out—to get her dad, rocker Rod Stewart, to drop her off a block from school. Her classmates ridiculed him for his attire and certain sexually related rumors. But by the time Kim turned sixteen, she felt as proud as a girl can be when she realized how popular her dad was (even if he was also unavailable for her). It's probably no coincidence that the daughter of a man infamous for having a "model of the month" hanging on his arm is now pursuing a modeling career herself (lest you think this is a onetime anomaly, Elizabeth Jagger, daughter of Rolling Stones' Mick Jagger, is also pursuing a modeling career).

One of the lowlights of "rock parenting" has to be the now-deceased John Phillips, who played for the Mamas and Papas. When his then thirteen-year-old daughter showed up at the door after having run away from her mom's house, John welcomed her in while holding a marijuana joint in his hand.

"What are the rules?" the barely adolescent Mackenzie asked.

"Well, let me see, You have to come home at least once a week. And if you come home from going out the night before and it's light out, always bring a change of clothing, because a lady is never seen during daylight hours wearing evening clothing."[3]

Mick Jagger was staying at Phillips's house the day Mackenzie came calling. The biggest Rolling Stone waited five years until Mackenzie turned 18, then one day he locked the door after Phillips left to get something at the store. He looked Mackenzie in the eyes and said, "I've been waiting to do this since you were ten years old."

When John returned and saw the locked door, he started banging on it, but all he offered was, "Mick, be nice to her! Don't hurt her." When Mackenzie replied, "Dad, leave us alone. It's fine," John walked away.

Amazingly, it gets worse. Once Mackenzie had a taste of Mick Jagger, John thought his daughter should also get her first taste of intravenous cocaine. He actually helped Mackenzie with her first injection. This appalled even Mick Jagger, but John explained to his fellow rocker, "You know what? Me and that kid have been friends for too long for me to hide anything from her."

Now that John is dead, Mackenzie, in her forties, can still get teary-eyed when she thinks of him. "He never looked back and said, 'I'm really sorry.' Never, never, never. But I miss him every day."[4]

I miss him every day. How do you miss a man who allows you to be sexually taken advantage of by a much older man? How do you miss a father who helps you to fall into one of the biggest life-wasting traps ever concocted, cocaine?

You miss him because he's your father. Even the worst of parents leaves such a profound mark on our souls that we will miss them when they're gone.

Both of us hear from many parents in a near panic about peer pressure, but the truth is, parents can exert a far greater influence—for good or for ill—if they'll just become more involved. *You* are the greatest influence in your kid's life.

Whether you agree with the sex ed your kid receives in elementary school matters less than the model you give him or her, especially during your child's most vulnerable times of the day: waking, struggling through homework, getting ready for school, or relaxing at the end of the day. Puberty education at home has everything to do with sex, and it has nothing to do with sex. It's what you say about sex and the physical affection you model with your spouse, but it's also about the home life you have in general. It's what transpires during the day. It's what you say when you get up, when you greet each other, or when you care for someone who's sick.

Someone once said that if you were to watch a movie of an average day in your life, you would go mad with boredom. An average day for most of us simply doesn't contain many explosions, car chases, or gun battles in abandoned warehouses. But God uses the very aspects that seem the most mundane to shape our lives and the lives of our kids. When it comes to sexuality and expressing what it means to be a man or a woman, your kids are going to draw from what they know best: Dad and Mom.

Your marriage informs your kid's sexuality more than anything else. If every day you treat each other like dirt, you give your kid a more damaging message than the worst video MTV can dish out. If Dad's always the macho man and Mom's the doormat, or Dad's the doormat and Mom's head honcho, then that's the model of sexuality that your kid is going to emulate.

You have power that MTV, Hollywood, and even your child's peers don't have: you can determine the amount of spending money a child has; you can set the basic routines of his or her day; and you can demonstrate how people should live in the most private parts of life.

Real Life

One of MTV's most popular and longest-running series is called *The Real World*. Actually, this show is anything *but* real life. Eight young people living together in one house, with cameras catching every conversation, looks as unlike real life as anything either of us could imagine.

Yet many kids watch that series and model their life accordingly. Your job as a parent is to model life as it actually is. Not life as your children's peers would have it, but life as you know it to be.

A good example is the growing pressure for parents to lose their minds when it comes to financing their kids' school-dance nights. Some kids spend over $1,000 on a single dance night! Consider this one example:

"For Dan Aversano, the Truck-ousine was the answer. With a Jacuzzi, two TVs, a VCR, a PlayStation, and room for 10, this elongated pickup he rented for his prom last spring topped the stretch Lexus the Mineola, New York, senior had taken to his junior prom. 'We were looking to do something more,' he says. 'My dad thought it was a little ridiculous. But I have to say, it was so much fun, I wish I could do it again.' After the prom, at a country club on Long Island's North Shore, Dan and his friends took off to a seven-bedroom house with a tennis court they rented in the Hamptons, a favorite vacation spot for celebrities. Dan's share of the prom costs: $1,000."[5]

How many *married couples* do you know that go even once a year on a date that costs $1,000 for a single night? That's not real life! Most parents I know think twice about dropping $75 to hire a babysitter, go to the movies, and eat at a fancy burger joint. Sadly, many kids today do spend almost a grand for their seventh-grade dances. When I try to challenge this, some parents will say to me, "Oh, Dr. Leman. If you can afford it, it's good for kids to have a little extravagant fun now and then."

We're saying this is *not* good for kids. It's crazy. It's destructive. It pushes them to grow up too fast, and it develops unrealistic concepts about budgeting.

Pubescence lasts only so long; don't make it shorter than it already is. The world is trying to fire up a jet engine on our kids' tails to rocket them into adulthood, but we want kids to grow up ASAP—as *slowly* as possible.

Here's the dilemma many parents miss, which in reality is the power behind most peer influence: Your boy or girl often wants desperately to be anyone except who he or she is. Kids want to stand out in one way (being popular and noticed), but they want to blend in as well (not drawing embarrassing attention, not being picked on). Our job as parents is to teach them how to become their own person rather than to define themselves by their peers' reactions.

"Be your own person" can be a hard sell to a pubescent who wants to be like everyone else. As a parent, the trick is to encourage your child to be one of a kind, a true original, and to let that child know she doesn't have to go along with everyone else's folly.

Now, if you dress your toddler up in designer clothes, you can't suddenly stop when they hit pubescence. We've met parents who give their three- and four-year-old kids stylish haircuts. Three- and four-year-old kids! What kind of a message does that send? That you want your kid to be like everyone else? You should want your kid to be himself or herself; everyone else's kid isn't doing all that great, in case you haven't noticed!

If you've established a healthy pattern, however, and have raised your kids not to go along with every fad and designer-clothing fetish that gets thrown our way every seven months, then your child *can* be different—in a good way. They'll see life as it really is.

We've found that parents are as vulnerable to peer pressure as their children. You're often the ones allowing your kids to go along with the pack because *you* want to keep up appearances. Before you tackle peer pressure in your kids, make sure you root it out of yourself!

This is important, because while peer pressure can be controlled, it remains a strong force.

Your Kid *Will* Struggle with This

"Okay, what's up?" Ann asked her daughter, Jennifer, during a day at the pool. The two had come to swim together, and Jennifer had been acting odd the entire time but wouldn't say why. Finally, after some patient parental prodding, Jennifer spoke up.

"See those girls over there?" Jennifer said, looking toward the Jacuzzi. "I know them from school." The two young women, looking immaculate in their perfect hair and precise makeup, sat across the pool in bikinis, flirting with some teenage boys. Jennifer, dressed in her Speedo and with her hair still dripping from her swim, looked back to her mother.

At first Ann felt surprised. The young men Jennifer had pointed to didn't seem the kind of boys Ann thought her daughter would choose; certainly they weren't the kind *she* would want Jennifer hanging out with. But rather than thinking, *Why are you having such a problem with this?* or, *I thought you were above this,* Ann opened the moment by asking Jennifer to consider where she would rather be.

After a long and meaningful conversation, Jennifer realized that her choice wasn't with the two pretentious debutantes. Mother and daughter left the pool, both of them knowing that the Jacuzzi life was not what Jennifer ultimately wanted.

Parents, you need to understand that even healthy and well-raised children will occasionally experience full-blown peer pressure, and this does not reflect on your skills as a parent. There will be moments when kids look around and think, *Doggone it, I wish I could do that,* even if it goes against what they know to be right.

We adults do the same. We look around and think, *Man, I wish I had his job!* Kids are going to struggle with it, too. But if you parent well, these moments of struggle will be *moments* of struggle, not months or years. Remember that the next time you see your kids struggling and you think, *I thought we raised you better than this.*

A Parent's Field Guide to the Mall: Don't Be Afraid to Walk

On a mother-daughter afternoon, Amy and I (Kathy) were shopping at the mall when we saw a "tweenager" daughter loudly telling her mother off. Amy watched in shock as the mother simply absorbed her daughter's lip.

Later I reminded Amy of our early days of shopping together. Though not to the same degree, Amy had disrespected me a few times at the mall, and I vowed never to let it happen again. In fact, after the first time it happened, I laid down the rule that any sign of disrespect in public was grounds to leave. "I'm here to do lunch," I told her before our next trip, "to shop until we drop, and to buy you things that you actually want." Then I added, "But if I say, 'No,' it is no. If I say, 'Yes,' it is yes. And if I say, 'Convince me,' then I'm giving you the opportunity to use your best sales pitch. But if you roll your eyes, shrug your shoulders, and carry on, I will turn around and meet you in the car." It took *three times* of leaving the mall prematurely before Amy learned that I meant what I had said.

Parents, after you've laid down the rules, don't be afraid to walk. It's your dollar, so you get to choose where you spend it. Skirts are getting shorter, and jeans are riding lower; if I don't like what I see, I don't buy it for my daughter. I'm surprised and frankly saddened when I see parents tied to their kid in the store because they don't understand that they can simply walk out when the manipulation starts. Some parents continue to argue or even cave in and begin writing the check, though doing so violates what they know is right. It doesn't do you any good, and indeed does considerable harm, when you bargain with your kids on something you've already made perfectly clear.

In one sense, this is a reverse form of peer pressure; the kids are influencing the parents! In such cases, adults let a group of pubescent kids determine what is appropriate and right.

Sometimes this parental cowardice comes cloaked in allegedly noble language. A father once told one of us, "I'm going to buy my daughter whatever she wants, because I remember striving to fit in among my peers and my own struggles with my parents over what clothes to buy." That father is doing his daughter an extreme disservice when it comes to her future personal financial management. How will she make the adjustment when the budget doesn't permit anything more than Wal-Mart?

Listen, if you don't take charge of this pressure to get more for your pubescent, it's only going to get far worse later on. The choices and issues only get more complicated. In just a few years, Suzie Q and Joe Cool will be asking for the car keys to head out on their dates. Will they want to drive the minivan? Not if they're accustomed to designer jeans and $250 Nike shoes. They *have* to drive the Lexus!

A good rule is this: look at your kid's demeanor now and multiply that by a few more years and a *lot* more attitude, and you'll have a pretty good picture of what life will be like when you're parenting an adolescent.

Work on setting boundaries and fostering respect while the issues are still manageable. That's the beauty of the puberty years. And these boundaries must extend not only to what our kids wear but to what they watch and listen to.

Media Mania

Dr. Leman has never been a big fan of either movies or television, but occasionally he'll pause to check up on what his daughters are watching. On one occasion, he caught them looking at one of the latest "reality" TV shows.

"That is a *lie,*" he said. "What you just heard was really a lie."

This was followed by a more in-depth discussion of why what the girls just saw was a lie and why their father so forcefully disagreed with the view of life that was being presented.

If his daughters are watching something inappropriate, usually Dr. Leman will simply turn off the TV. But sometimes—and this is key—he'll watch such a program with his daughters for the purpose of talking to them about it.

On one occasion, Hannah fell under the spell of *The Bachelor.*

"Honey," Dr. Leman said, "let me tell you why this relationship isn't going to work. One guy can't possibly spend just six weeks 'courting' twenty-five women and be able to make any kind of intelligent decision. It's a ridiculous premise to begin with."

"But what if they took longer?" Hannah asked.

"Six weeks, thirteen weeks—what's the difference? My friend Neil Clark Warren says that if you're going to get serious about somebody, you should plan to date that person for at least *two years,* while you're living in the same town. The reason for the proximity is that you can hide every addiction known to mankind by dating sporadically from afar. You'll never really know a guy, Hannah, until you've lived in the same city with him for at least six or seven seasons."

During the final episode, the bachelor actually ended up proposing, but Dr. Leman wasn't buying it. He told Hannah, "I'd put twenty dollars on their noses that they aren't going to make it. When I hear him say, 'This is the woman I want to share my life with, I want to be with her forever,' it makes me laugh. He hasn't smelled her bad breath. He hasn't had to clean up her hurl."

"Dad!"

"Well, honey, it's true. There are times I've had to hold your mother's hair out of the way while she got sick in the toilet. This living in a penthouse and going on elaborate dates won't tell you squat about each other. It's so tinsel-like; and kids, of course, fall prey to tinsel. Listen: there's nothing instantaneous about relationships. Only a very shallow society thinks otherwise."

"Do you think these people are shallow?"

"Yes, honey, I do."

When the announcement came, virtually days later, that the couple had split up, Dr. Leman's words were proven true.

I report this incident, assuming that involved parents will take the time to experience media *with* their children; it's simply irresponsible these days to abandon your children to the television set or even the radio and not pay attention to what's going into their brains. We're not just talking about gratuitous sex and violence; just as damaging are the false notions of love and romance that many so-called reality shows promote.

Kathy held a Valentine's Day dance for her daughter Amy and Amy's girlfriends when Amy was in fifth grade. Kathy set up streamers and provided the pink punch. The girls dressed up in their pretty dresses, and they decorated their own cookies. Amy's friends brought some of their own music and danced in the living room while Kathy watched with another mother.

Kathy recalls, "As I sat there, it was amazing to see which girls were doing gyrations on the floor. I never even knew their mothers let them buy the music they had. I made a mental note: *Kathy, next time you think you know somebody, think twice.* Though at that point Amy didn't realize what the other girls were doing by their gyrations, I thought, *Girl, we need to talk.*"

The Kaiser Family Foundation found that "sixty-eight percent of all [TV] shows include sexual content, up from 56 percent in 97/98. . . . The most widely viewed shows—those airing in primetime on the major broadcast networks—are even more likely to include sexual content. Three out of four of these shows include sexual content, up from two out of three during the 97/98 season."[6] As if that weren't enough, "24 percent of teens 12 to 17 years old say they would like more information about sex and relationships from TV."[7]

To talk openly with your pubescent, you will need to familiarize yourself with what your teen gets exposed to daily. To do this, you will have to read their magazines, listen to their radio stations, and watch their movies. Ratings don't mean squat these days; if you allowed your thirteen-year-old to go unaccompanied three times to the PG-13 movie *Titanic*, for instance, in our opinion you made a big mistake!

If you think your child is protected, you are probably wrong. Your child sits in your car reading billboards. Your child walks with you through the grocery-store checkout aisle with its tabloid covers. Your child associates with other children his age whose parents do not protect them as much as you think they do. Once your child leaves home, he will encounter a very different world. After getting a taste of the real world, some children will look at you, their parents, and think you live in a cave and decide they cannot talk to a Dad or a Mom so obviously out of it. Other children will still come home, but with their minds full of questions. Much depends on the track record you've built with your child.

As a result of Amy's Valentine's Day party, Kathy realized that when her kids weren't with her, they would be exposed to radio stations she didn't approve of. So she told them, "If there's a way you can move yourself into another room, then do that. If there's a way to engage yourself in conversation that distracts you from the music, do what you can."

Thankfully, her kids have learned to take responsibility for themselves. While visiting relatives in Phoenix, the Bell family stopped by Blockbuster Video to rent a movie. When the kids couldn't find a suitable one, they left empty-handed. Kathy admits, "We were proud of them!"

Puppy-Love Pressure

There's yet another kind of peer pressure: puppy love. It can be the most enthralling pressure of all.

In western New York where Dr. Leman grew up, square dancing was part of the P.E. curriculum. One day they lined up all the girls alphabetically on one side of the gym and all the boys about twenty feet away on the other side. Dr. Leman can remember it like it was yesterday:

We stared at each other dumbly, as seventh and eighth graders do.

"Okay, girls," our gym teacher said, "I want you to pick a partner. Anybody will do."

A girl named Marci walked up to me, blonde and smiling. I was in seventh grade, and she was an eighth grader, another species entirely. *An older woman!*

"Would you like to dance with me?" she asked.

Holy kamoley! I thought. *She's in eighth grade—and she's got a bra!*

"Shuurrr—err," I said, my voice lurching like a popped clutch.

My friends and I were dumber than mud, as boys often are. During these dances we would surreptitiously run our thumbs up the girls' backs to probe for bras ("bra checks," we called them). But that afternoon after P.E. class, I felt I had left behind my childish ways as I sat doodling her name on a pad of paper: *Marci.* And then, for good measure, I added my last name, as if trying on a wedding band.

These moments of pubescent euphoria bring the first hints of puppy love. The pubescent child certainly walks and thinks a little differently. Just be careful that you don't ascribe adolescent thinking to a pubescent's feeling.

In the movie *My Fair Lady,* Freddie feels smitten with Eliza Doolittle. He croons, "I have often walked down this street before, but the pavement always stayed beneath my feet before. All at once am I several stories high, knowing I'm on the street where you live."

Puppy love is kind of like that. It's the first feeling that you "like" someone and that someone "likes" you—someone other than Dad and Mom. It's like the euphoria of knowing deep down that your parents love you, but you now realize that that's not the end, that there is more out there. A kid who is deeply loved by his parents probably isn't going to stumble, because of the sea of support and love that surrounds him.

Puppy love is a natural part of maturation, because puberty brings kids a growing awareness of the opposite sex. Adults may ask, "Do you have a boyfriend or a girlfriend?" but this is not something either of us recommend asking, as it encourages the whole process in a not-so-subtle manner. Pubescents don't need us to wake them up; their bodies will take care of that!

"No, I don't like boys or girls," a child in early pubescence might say. When they get a little closer to adolescence, that'll change to, "Hey, find out if she likes me."

Around the time your child reaches fourth or fifth grade, you'll hear things such as "They're going together." In most cases, all that means is that they "like" each other. It's the initial stage of puppy love. Kids at that age are shallow at best and are impressed with the tinseled life.

Take it in stride. Don't overreact to it. Teachable moments will abound, such as when your ten-year-old daughter tells you that a boy likes her. She might add, "I hate him! He's such a jerk," which is a very typical reaction for a little girl.

You might say, "Honey, listen. I know what you're saying. You're saying you don't like him for one reason or another. You're going to meet all kinds of people in life, and some of them are easier to like than others. But it's good to look for the good things in people. Even if you don't like him, what are some things about him that are nice?"

"Nothing! There's not a single good thing about him."

"Well, how does he do in school?"

"He's one of those smart ones that gets all A's."

"Well, there's something. He's obviously a good student. He's just immature, and some of the things he does to get your attention, believe it or not, just might be ways that he's trying to tell you that he likes you."

"Why would he keep pushing me if he likes me?"

"Listen, I've been there and done that. That's one of the ways that a little boy tells a little girl that he likes her."

"By pushing her?"

"By pushing her. Isn't that weird? Honey, boys are weird, and they get even weirder than that."

Every parent wants to be a teacher to his or her child, and here's your chance to put yourself in that place. But if you say, *"What* did you say?! You're *going* with him? Let's get one thing straight: you are *not* dating until you are at least seventeen years old and have your father's approval and mine!" Well, you've just made a massive leap across a chasm as wide as the Grand Canyon. That's what we mean by ascribing adolescent emotions to a pubescent child. Find out what "going together" means to your child and deal with it on that basis rather than jump to conclusions.

Puppy love is a common part of growing up; take it all in stride to keep it in perspective. To your kid it may feel very ego-fulfilling, as if he's on top of the world. But you can help ground him by not making more out of it than it is.

In addition to puppy-love passion, which usually lasts about half as long as any professional sport season, you'll find your pubescent trying to survive the pressure from peer relationships. You can help take some of this pressure off by guiding your child into healthy, encouraging relationships.

Friends

"Mom, can Sally come over?" your daughter calls from the kitchen phone.

"Sure," you reply.

A couple of minutes pass, and your daughter's high voice breaks the silence once more. "Her mom can bring her over, but she can't take her home."

"Honey, I'll be glad to take her home," you reply.

Making such a trip may inconvenience you, but it's an inconvenience that's well worth it. By way of your actions, you're putting a premium on your child. What's the message to your kid? "Mom cares about me, and she cares about my friendships." Does that mean that every time a kid asks for something, you should drop everything and go do it? No, of course not. Sometimes you'll have to say, "Honey, I'd love to have Sally over. But unfortunately, Uncle Roger and Aunt Helen are coming for the afternoon and I've got to get ready."

"But Mom . . ."

"Honey, we'll do it another time."

Like you, we want our children to develop friendships; we want them to learn how to be a good friend. How do you encourage good friendships? It goes back to what we talked about earlier, about your house being a home and not a hotel. Your home should be a center for your kid's activity.

Admittedly, this opens up many messy realities, but when these little disappointments happen in your home, you're far better equipped to deal with them. Kids aren't always nice to each other. They're selfish and hedonistic by nature, and there will probably come a time when your kid tears up because of what someone said. Don't be afraid to tell your children the truth: all sorts of people in life will use you and abuse you. Some people will say they are your friend when they really aren't.

I (Dr. Leman) talked with a professional football coach who was scouting a player at the University of Arizona. I told him about one excellent player I knew—and he really was good—and this coach said something interesting. "There are a lot of good ball players," he said, "but only a few can play on Sunday afternoon."

That speaks of life to me. Many people claim to be your friend, but only a few are really going to stick by you. I have three close male friends; one is my best friend with whom I can talk about anything. The other two will drop whatever they're doing if I call.

Most adults don't have three friends. When you find a deep, mutual camaraderie, hold fast to them and nurture them. Your kids need to see that friendships are an important part of life.

We've talked about puppy love and peer relationships, but the most important relationship during your child's puberty is the parent-child relationship. You'll be called to find the delicate balance of seizing the day without seizing the reins.

Seize the Day, Not the Reins

The story has become a familiar one to me (Dr. Leman) in my counseling practice: parents come in with their thirteen-year-old daughter who is an early bloomer in every sense of the word—physically, emotionally, and in her mind, relationally. She thinks she's "ready for the boy scene."

First the good news: these parents care enough to involve themselves in their daughter's life. Now the bad news: they freak out and clamp down on her, overcontrol her, and overparent her. They are what I call hover parents.

Unfortunately, this reaction is all too common. Many parents don't act in authority; they act as dictators. "Hey, you are going to do what I tell you to do as long as you live under this roof! And you get that look off your face, or I'll change it for you!" If you hover over a kid and become an authoritarian parent, one who makes all the decisions for your child, you're in for trouble. A pubescent needs a bit of room to grow; an adolescent needs even more. If you don't loosen up their reins, you'll set the stage for a serious rebellion.

I realize that such advice may step on some parents' toes. You may be thinking, *Are you saying my child knows better than I do?* Certainly not. But my point is this: what message does a hover parent send to his child? Namely, "Mom and I do not think you know how to make it in this world. We believe you're completely incompetent, so we're going to continue treating you like a toddler."

That's a bitter pill to swallow, day after day, for a human being trying in every way to grow up. The art of parenting is a subtle one: you must gradually, in the right proportion, loosen your hold on the reins and let your child begin to run.

Of course, you can let go too far, too fast! We've both met parents at the other end of the spectrum who, in essence, say, "Honey, I want to meet your every need. I want to make sure you're happy, happy, happy." No matter what the child asks for, they get it. A grotesquely violent video game? No problem. A rap album with lewd lyrics? Absolutely. Clothes that reveal half of their daughter's derriere? Sure; after all, it's just a phase.

What this type of parent is communicating comes down to, "You're already fully equipped for the world, so I'm going to give you license to call the shots. You just let me know what you need to keep growing, and I'll pull out my credit card."

Well, the truth is, a pubescent kid *doesn't* know what he or she needs. If your kid calls you a "no-good-son-of-a-beep," you certainly wouldn't say, "Oh, honey, I'm sensing that you're upset with me." You shouldn't take that from your kid under any circumstance. They need to know that there's a price to be paid for getting lippy.

But that doesn't mean you want your house to resemble a work camp, either. There's a balance between being *laissez faire* to the point that your kids aren't held accountable and the other extreme of being so authoritarian that you practically map out their life.

Both extremes will produce rebellion. As a parent, you walk a balance beam of life: don't overreact, don't underreact; otherwise, what will that kid do at thirteen? She'll become a wild child—running away, sneaking out at night, getting into drugs, and getting pregnant at sixteen. We see it happen all the time.

There's something wonderful about being what I (Dr. Leman) call an authoritative parent. That's *authoritative,* one who stays in healthy authority over a child, not *authoritarian,* one who bellows out demands. I base this on Ephesians 6, which begins, "Children obey your parents in the Lord, for this is right." God has placed you in healthy authority over your children.

The pressure boiling inside your kid comes down to this: he wants to grow but doesn't know the way yet; he still needs your guidance. Your kid isn't going to tell you that in so many words, but that's what he's feeling.

What's the healthy way to respond in such a situation? Create age-appropriate boundaries. Your pubescent child should have more freedom than a toddler but less than an adolescent. They can listen to certain styles of music, but you can veto any album based on its lyrics. They can choose their activities, but you get to limit the amount of time they are away from home. They can choose their own clothing, but you can veto inappropriate outfits.

Boundaries are healthy; but narrow, straight lines without any turns are unhealthy. In that kind of environment, your kid is going to feel like she's in a prison, not a house, and she'll spend most of her day plotting her escape. Your child is in that middle ground between childhood and adulthood, and she needs both parental guidance and the personal freedom to exercise some responsibility.

Is it easy to find this balance? Hardly. But it's crucial that you strive for it.

Positive Peer Pressure: The Family

It has been proven that pubescent kids will violate their own consciences to gain acceptance into a peer group. That's why some kids join gangs. That's why others dress like hookers and still others pierce their face with all manner of metal.

But a kid usually does this only when he doesn't feel like he belongs anywhere else. We've hinted at this already, so we don't want to belabor the point, but it would be irresponsible of us to complete this chapter without stressing the best defense against peer pressure: family belonging.

When your kid feels he belongs to your family, he has little reason—from a psychological perspective, anyway— to engage in aberrant behavior. That's a strong statement, but it's true. Healthy kids want to fit into healthy families. They love being with their family and feel more concerned about doing something that would upset that bond than they are about fitting in with a group at school.

How do you get kids to feel they're part of the family? Is it simply by saying wonderful words, praising them, telling them how wonderful they are? No, kids see through that in a nanosecond. You do it by *letting that child give back to the family*. If you want a responsible child at sixteen, you have to begin granting him responsibility and choices and building in accountability at ages six, seven, and eight.

You also create a sense of belonging by spending time together, not just as an immediate family but as an extended one. Dr. Mary Pipher says, "One of the best things for a nine-year-old is having her spend a lot of time with grandparents, cousins and so on—people who value her for something besides how sexy and popular she is."[8]

When a girl knows her grandmother and her grandmother knows her, when she looks forward to seeing her dad every night and has meaningful conversations with her mother, when she realizes that she matters at home and that she contributes to the health and welfare of her family, she is about as free from the allure of peer pressure as a child can be.

It's a cliché, but it's true: you can curse the darkness (peer pressure) or you can light a candle (create a sense of belonging at home). It's our hope that you'll light a candle.

Make Your Kid Your Hero

How to Be a Positive Influence in Your Pubescent's Life

As a third grader, Mike Carroll wrote an essay titled "When I Grow Up." It began like this: "When I grow up I will be a fireman like my father.... If I were a fireman like my father, I would help put out fires, go around the building to see if people were trapped, and I would try to save them. I admire my father."[1]

Michael's ambition proved to be more than an eight-year-old's fantasy. After graduating from college in 1984, Mike briefly held an office job but soon found that the nine-to-five world wasn't one he wanted to inhabit. He became one of 30,000 people who took the physical test for the New York Fire Department and finished in the top 600.

Calling this ordeal a "test" is sort of like calling World War II a disagreement. Since so many people eagerly want to join the fire department, the application process and physical requirements border on cruelty, in the department's fierce determination to weed out the weak. Put it this way: the year Mike took the test, *three men died taking it*. The would-be firemen have to carry hoses, hoist ladders, transport heavy dummies, and get over, through, and under obstacles. Just when their mental and physical exertion has reached its limit, they're told to work their way through a pitch-black, claustrophobic's nightmare of a tunnel. Not only do they have to survive this; if they want to make it into the fire department, their time has to be better than most of the other 30,000 people trying to get in.

It took a couple of years for Mike's time to earn him a place in the department (applicants are hired by their ranking), but eventually he got in, just like his dad and just like his brother—both of whom "made a few calls" and got Michael into Ladder 3, where Michael's dad had served for twenty-two years and where Michael's brother ended up staying for twenty years.

Michael served with distinction—on and off the force. His captain chose him to be the "chauffeur," firefighter-speak for the guy a captain chooses to drive the rig and to stay by his side, discussing strategy and essentially acting as the top assistant. Not only was Michael a top firefighter, but he also played a key role on Ladder 3's softball team. If you think the major leagues seem competitive, you haven't watched competing firehouses play for the championship.

Michael was on duty in early September 2001. On September 9, his wife, Nancy, brought Michael's two young kids—six-year-old Brendan and three-year-old Olivia—to the firehouse for a family get-together. They got to sit in the truck and slide down the pole, and though they couldn't stay long because they had school the next day, it would soon become a time that the wife and children would never forget. It was the last time they ever saw Michael alive.

On September 11, Michael answered a call to put out a fire at the World Trade Center. The north tower was the first building hit by a terrorist-driven plane, and Michael and his buddies soon found themselves on the forty-fourth floor, getting people outside to safety.

As the world watched the terrible events taking place that day, Michael's wife went through her own, more personal ordeal. She could see the disaster unfolding on television, and Michael's brother called her to confirm her husband's role. "He's working," Michael's brother said.

Nancy remained silent.

"It's just a fire now," Michael's brother tried to console her. "They'll put the fire out. That's what they do."

It's what Michael had dreamed of doing since the third grade when he wrote in his essay, "I would help put out fires, go around the building to see if people were trapped, and I would try to save them."

At 10:00 A.M., the south tower collapsed. Michael and his fellow firemen heard what happened and recognized their own desperate peril. The captain radioed in that the north tower also appeared about to go down. Michael stood right by the captain's side.

Minutes later, the north tower collapsed, taking Michael, his captain, and most of his buddies with him. It took almost three months to dig Michael's body out of the rubble. Workers found him lying close by his captain's side.

Michael's brother, Bill, delivered the eulogy at Michael's memorial service, which was attended by more than 1,500 people. Few will ever forget Bill's last sentence: "Godspeed my brother, my friend, my hero."

Every kid wants to be a hero, and in the wake of those terrible attacks on September 11, our country became vividly aware of the many "common heroes" living in our midst. Boys dream about serving as firemen and rescuing people from burning buildings, of flying to another planet to establish a colony, or of pitching the final strike in game seven of the World Series. Girls dream of caring for the sick, of writing the next great American novel, or of scoring the winning goal in a World Cup soccer shoot-out. But as much as kids may crave the world's spotlight, if they could choose only one set of eyes to see them as heroes, that honor would go to you, their parent.

Your child craves your words of love and affirmation in those pubescent years, when chaotic physical development makes her feel she has all the grace of Mr. Potato Head. For her, talk is anything but cheap; she longs to hear words filled with admiration.

Imagine what it would mean for you as an adult to hear your own father or mother say, "I am still so blessed to have you as my child, and I'm happy to be with you in this journey of life!" Many people would like nothing more than to hear the words spoken at Mike Carroll's memorial service: "Godspeed my brother, my friend, my hero."

If this is true for us as adults, how much more so for kids who almost desperately look to their parents for daily cues on everything, from whether Mom noticed that her son swept the kitchen floor to whether her daughter cleaned the bathroom counters?

Don't take this job glibly. Your kid will sense a microwaved, stale speech, just as he'll recognize home-cooked encouragement. Your child may be ten or fourteen or eight, but he or she may be able to do things that you couldn't do at his or her age, or still can't do! You may have a difficult time speaking in public, but your eight-year-old daughter may be ready for her own television talk show. The only instrument you play may be the radio, but your nine-year-old son may be a concert violinist in the making. You may have trouble keeping up with the family dog during your walks around the neighborhood, but your twelve-year-old daughter may hold the third-fastest time on the middle school cross-country team. Where does your child shine? What do you admire about your child? Don't hold your admiration inside! Let it flow!

But don't stop there; focus on character also. Tell your son how he stands out for his compassion. Point out to your daughter her gift for inviting conversation, something you've been working toward for years.

The thought that she has been gifted with something you haven't may amaze her.

Why is making your kid your hero important when it comes to sex ed? Because as one high school virgin put it, "Boys make you feel like you're special and you're the only one they care about. A lot of girls feel like they need that. But my mother loves me and my father loves me, so there's no gap to fill."[2]

Catch Your Kids Doing Something Right

Nine-year-old Cody and his six-year-old brother, Shane, thought they were minding their own business. Imagine their surprise when Lincoln County Sheriff John Coley pulled them over on their bicycles.

It's one thing to get in trouble with your teacher, or even with the principal—but the county sheriff? How would the boys explain *this* to their parents? Getting busted by the police does not bode well for allowance raises or after-dinner desserts.

The boys got "cited" for wearing bike helmets; their "fine" consisted of coupons for free ice cream! The incident occurred as part of a special bike-safety-awareness program, now practiced in various forms throughout North America. The program uses rewards to reinforce good behavior and create a positive first encounter with police.[3]

We loved reading about this because, frankly, kids often make a career out of getting caught. One afternoon it's talking back to Mom about washing the dishes; the next it's leaving the hose running on a hot summer's day. One evening it's staying too long at a friend's house and coming home late for dinner; the next it's picking on a little sister.

Pointing out kids' mistakes is all part of discipline, but when was the last time you caught your kid doing something right? If discipline is more closely related to discipleship than to punishment, it will involve all aspects of your child's life—*the good as well as the bad.* So when you see your daughter doing something right, tell her! Pull her aside on the sly, and say, "You know, for what it's worth, I'm impressed with how you dealt with that. You're really growing up and handling tough situations." When you take the time to do this, you're depositing valuable affirmation and encouragement as she grows in maturity and responsibility. You're not saying, "I love you *because* you did this." You're just pointing out how well she's navigating the waters of life. Kids gather a lot of self-esteem when parents notice the good decisions they make and say, "Good for you!"

Not only is it important for your home to be a place where your children get caught succeeding; your home must also become a place where kids learn to fail. When you consider your own life, did you learn more from success or from failure? Usually the bumps and bruises along the way teach us the most valuable lessons.

A list in Dr. Leman's book *The New Birth Order Book* points out the difference between pursuers of excellence and perfectionists. Perfectionists—those who haven't learned how to fail and obsess on avoiding it—have standards far too high, while pursuers of excellence have high standards that remain within reach. The perfectionist hates criticism; the pursuer of excellence welcomes it. As you let your kids fail, you teach them to be responsible. And a responsible kid will be less apt to get himself into trouble with drugs and sex.

Dr. Leman graduated fourth in his high school class—fourth from the bottom, that is. A lot of people wrote him off, but John and May Leman didn't. When a parent believes in a kid, even though the school guidance counselor has filed him away as the village (or school) idiot, it makes a world of difference. Your encouragement and affirmation can make a huge difference in your kid's life! Dr. Leman freely admits, "I would not be where I am today were it not for the love and support, the strong values, and Christian commitment of my parents." Parents who say "Good for you!" are looking out for their kids' best interests. They build their son up when the rest of the world tears him down. They take the time to point out their daughter's specific strengths. And they aren't afraid to have their kid take responsibility for his or her own actions, even if it means stepping back when they most want to step in and take over.

"I believe in you," "I trust you," "I think the best of you"—these phrases all make excellent tools for encouraging our pubescent children.

And consider yet another aspect of this. So often we parents look at the negative rather than the positive of a situation that could be interpreted either way. When my daughter, Lizzie Bell, was six years old, she received an invitation to speak about her rare bone-marrow disease. There we met Greg LeMond and his wife, Kathy. Greg LeMond was the first American to ever win the Tour de France, the world's most prestigious bicycle race.

Greg revealed that when he was just learning to ride and race competitively, he couldn't find a bike that fit him, so he started tearing up bikes and created his own. How many parents would look at their kid and get excited that he tore up bikes? Most would object, "Do you know how much I paid for that? Have you lost your mind?!"

Greg has become famous for the "LeMond bike" only because he decided to get creative and make something better than what he found out there. Greg's stunning upset victory (after he recovered from a gunshot accident, no less) in the 1989 Tour de France was due in part to his ingenuity. He lagged a formidable fifty seconds behind the leader going into the final time trial—a hurdle that nobody thought he could make up. But Greg wore a specially designed, aerodynamic helmet, while his competitor, Laurent Fignon, rode with a flopping ponytail. Greg used a special disk for the back wheel instead of spokes, a cutting-edge innovation at the time. And he had worked to develop new handlebars that kept his elbows tucked in, reducing drag.

Those innovations, together with a heart bigger than the state of Texas, brought Greg to the finish line fifty-eight seconds ahead of Fignon's time, which meant he won the twenty-one-day race by the slimmest margin ever, a mere eight seconds.

Greg had planted the seeds of his fantastic victory years before in his garage when he tore up several bikes to create a better one. Greg LeMond was a leader, and leaders often upset the status quo. If you're a status-quo parent, always doing things by the book and never thinking outside the box, you can do great damage to a creative, resourceful child when you look at the negative ("He's tearing up his bike!") instead of the positive ("He's showing great initiative and creativity").

The Body Villain

Negative parents—those who never take the time to catch their children doing something right—often increase the psychological damage by also passing on a revulsion of the body's natural processes. Some kids learn early to feel ashamed of their bodies, and many of them never quite shake the harmful lesson. When I (Kathy) teach my parent classes, I still hear women say, "I'm embarrassed about my body. I hate my butt. I walk into the shower backward because I don't want my husband looking at my rear end."

This message gets passed on to kids early in their childhood. "Who passed the gas? You really stink," adults may say. "You have crusties coming out of your eyes—clean your face!" By the time kids reach puberty, they've obviously gotten the message, because when I tell them that they'll begin growing hair in their armpits, they say, "Oooh, yuck!" even though those hair shafts play an integral role in our bodies, collecting perspiration and helping to keep us cool. When I tell girls, "You will begin having yellow mucus on your underwear," they respond with a resounding "Gross!" Yet that mucus helps the vagina stay clean and free from disease. If our bodies didn't do these things, we'd have serious medical problems.

By puberty, many kids have already disassociated from their own bodies, and the changes they're facing seem to distance them further. "Okay," I'll say, "let's back up. These are all messages from your body that you're growing up. Every orifice in your body will have something coming out of it: your ears, your mouth, your nose, your eyes. Your vagina isn't any different than any other opening of your body; it's got to have moisture to keep it clean. This is all part of the plan."

It's so sad that what is actually a wonder of creation—God's beautiful design—gets turned into something dirty and shameful. You can help your pubescent children better accept their sexual development by ascribing dignity to their changing body functions. As kids learn to appreciate their God-given bodies, what may once have seemed repulsive may be seen for the gift that it is. Without your daughter's menstrual cycle, she would never enjoy the thrill of giving birth. Our children's attitude needs to change from "Gross!" to "Isn't that interesting? How do I take care of that part of my body?" or "Okay, that part of my body does smell; what should I do about it?"

Parents, you need to understand that if you don't provide a positive interpretation of bodily functions, your pubescent children will likely feel shame and discouragement about the changes happening to their bodies. A nocturnal emission is messy. A menstrual cycle is painful and smelly. But those two processes create the miracle of conception and life. Your kids will feel the shame; your job is to point out the beauty.

While bodily embarrassments weigh heavily on our pubescent children's shoulders, another challenge is equally formidable: finding the avenue through which they can make their greatest contribution. Kids with a sense of purpose and mission are far less likely to become sexually promiscuous.

Slow and Fat: The Recipe for Great Success!

Do the names Jerry Greenfield and Ben Cohen ring a bell? Perhaps not. But how about Ben and Jerry?

Yes, the ice cream guys.

By their own admission, Ben and Jerry were the two "slowest, fattest kids" in the seventh-grade gym class at Merrick Avenue Junior High.[4] They had both tried to make it in other fields but had failed and were looking for success elsewhere.

Sitting on the front steps of Jerry's parents' house in Merrick, Long Island, they finally narrowed it down to bagels or ice cream. Since they didn't have $40,000 for the necessary bagel-making equipment, ice cream started looking awfully good.

"We found an ad for a $5 ice-cream-making correspondence course offered through Penn State," they wrote. "Due to extreme poverty, we decided to split one course between us, sent in our five bucks, read the material they sent back, and passed the open-book tests with flying colors."[5]

Ice cream it was.

The two young men gathered $8,000, borrowed another $4,000, and with only a handful of supporters, set up shop in one of the few places they could find—an old gas station in Vermont, which is not exactly a tropical paradise during winter.[6]

How many people would have thought Ben and Jerry could make it? But they did! And it all started with two fat kids who tore up a gas station because they were too poor to make bagels.

What does the future hold for *your* kids?

One day as we drove to school, I (Kathy) asked my kids what they wanted to be when they grow up. "We want to be teachers, Mommy," my girls responded.

"You're going to be great teachers, if you do," I said. "You might teach in a school. You might teach on a reservation. You might even get married and become a mommy and teach your own children. We don't know where God is going to put you to show people his love."

"Lizzie," I asked, "what are some of Alicia's gifts?"

"Well," Lizzie said, "manners."

"That is something Alicia has learned," I clarified. "But that's not what Mommy's talking about. What is unique about Alicia that God just gave her as a little girl, without her having to do anything?"

Every gift from God provides a means to partner with him in his ministry to the world, and I wanted to get them wondering, *Why did God give me the gifts he did?* I wanted them to appreciate not only their own gifts but also the gifts of others. As we passed the grocery store, I had an idea.

"I want you to look in there," I said. "See that man mopping the floor? He's one of God's servants. God is watching and thinking, *Wow! Just look at my servant!*" As I spoke, I whooped it up in the car. "Look at how he's mopping that floor! Man, he is showing love because he cares, because he takes his time and reaches every nook and cranny, every crack in the floor; he's doing a great job. That's where God put him to show the world God's love."

We drove a bit further and I said, "See that trailer? There's an old man in there wearing diapers right now, and the only person who takes care of him is his son. Everyday his son loves his father by washing him and changing his diapers. And God is saying, 'Yeah!'"

"Then he sees Britney Spears," I said as we drove on, "and he says, 'You know, I gave her a great voice. I gave her the ability to dance. I gave her beauty. But what is she doing with it?' Is Britney glorifying God? Is she any more special because her stage is on television and before tens of thousands of fans? Is she any more important than the man who's changing his father's diapers? Britney has her stage, but helping his father is that man's stage."

What are your kid's gifts, her God-given characteristics intrinsic to her personality—beauty, strength, intelligence, compassion? What are your son's talents and abilities? How do they make him a special person? How might God use these gifts for his kingdom?

In the church the Bells attend, there is no question whether members will take some responsibility within the community; the question is, "What will it be?" Everyone is asked to do something, whether it's ushering, bringing up the gifts, singing in the choir, or carrying the cross. Every kid is encouraged to get involved. "Look around," we say, "see what the jobs are and which one you might like." It's something we've said to our kids since they were tiny. Some little kids have outstanding voices; that is their gift. It's something they could not go out and buy—which is a good way to talk to your kids about gifts. What do your kids have that no one can buy? What is there simply by the grace of God?

In the Leman household, we stress creating opportunities for our kids to give back to the family. Everyone brings something to our dinner table that no one else has; each person has his or her place. When kids have confidence that they are special, that they have a stage to be on in this life, that they have gifts given by God, they'll feel more confident with others who have different gifts. They will be able to acknowledge to others, "Wow, you are good. I really admire your gift and appreciate that you're using it well."

Each person is here on this earth for a reason. Among the millions of combinations that existed between sperm and egg to make one human being, your child was chosen. Despite what life feels like sometimes, there is a plan!

"There is something in this world," we need to tell our kids, "that only you can do."

You should be aware that it might be difficult for you to pick up on your child's strengths if you and your child have different personality types. Parents often don't realize how these personality differences can enormously influence their ability to affirm and relate to their child and his or her uniqueness. As you can imagine, many reasons exist for the differences among personalities, too many for us to deal with in depth here. But Dr. Leman urges parents to embrace the personality type of their kid in *The New Birth Order Book*. Those traits in your child that you sometimes think of as weaknesses may simply be the emerging strengths of a different personality type. Ask yourself, *Who am I? Who is my daughter? What are our potential sources of conflict? How can we work together? What is required for her success?*

Identifying and being aware of your differences can make the difference between a strained relationship and a strong relationship. What you see as odd (tearing apart a bike or being fat and slow in gym class) may just be the seeds for great success. What you see as annoying (being very talkative, overly analytical, a goof-off) may in fact be the very characteristics that help your kids excel in life.

The Hero

We started this chapter talking about heroes. Let's end it the same way. There's more to tell of Mike Carroll, the fireman who died in the World Trade Center.

Since he was a boy, Michael had a favorite baseball team: the New York Mets. Michael had a favorite player, too: Mike Piazza, the Mets' catcher. When Michael took his son, Brendan, to the batting cages to teach him how to hit, he used Piazza as the model to follow. Brendan— a Yankees fan—tried to hit like Derek Jeter, who waves his bat in the air with his hands held high. Michael told him to follow Piazza's practice of keeping his hands low and still.

Michael must have been crying happy tears in heaven the day before Thanksgiving 2001, when Mike Piazza knocked on the Carroll's door. A friend had told Piazza about Michael Carroll and his family, and without making any headlines, Piazza quietly agreed to pay a visit to Michael's widow and two children.

Piazza patiently answered Brendan's many questions, such as, "What's the Mets' clubhouse like?"

"It's a dump."

Brendan told the All-Star, "You were my dad's favorite player," and Piazza kept the emphasis where it belonged by responding, "That's a great honor."

Then Piazza took Brendan to the batting cage and showed him the Piazza way of hitting the ball. When Brendan took a hit on his hands from one of the balls, Mike Piazza sat next to him, rubbing out the soreness. "You'll be all right, buddy," he said. "You'll be all right."

Was he talking about the pitch or about life?

In his wildest dreams, Michael Carroll probably never could have imagined his son being consoled by Mike Piazza. And certainly he couldn't have imagined Mike Piazza not wanting the day to end and suggesting that Brendan come back to his place. Imagine that boy in his father's favorite player's home, holding his own in a video game as he sat on Mike Piazza's leather couch and looked at Mike Piazza's wide-screen television.

Nancy—Michael's widow—didn't have to wonder. "Mike's howling," she confidently told *Sports Illustrated* reporter Michael Bamberger. "Brendan is hanging out with Mike Piazza, in Mike Piazza's apartment, and Mike thinks it's the funniest thing in the world."[7]

Our kids want to be heroes, and they want us to be their heroes. You don't have to be a fireman or a professional athlete to fill that bill. You just have to notice your kids, encourage them, catch them doing something right, and appreciate them. If you'll do this, you'll create a very high and effective wall between them and some hustler or bimbo willing to give your daughter or son all the adulation they never received at home—as long as your daughter or son will grant them sexual favors in return.

Chapter 6

Kitchen-Table Sex Ed

After her mother died, my (Kathy's) grandmother—Rose Rodriquez—was raised in a convent along with her seven sisters and thus grew up among nuns who didn't talk about sex. Since nobody had ever talked to my grandmother about sex, she never talked to my mom about it, and that created trouble.

When my baton-twirling mom fell in love with my father—a high school football star—they were two poverty-stricken kids searching for love, forced by their parents' silence to find things out on their own. When Mom got pregnant, Dad asked the question still asked today: "Is it mine?" Mom put her hand on a Bible and swore that she hadn't been with anyone else.

Because she had to find out everything on her own, the hard way, my mother was determined that we would grow up knowing more than she had. Consequently, she delivered excellent "kitchen-table sex ed."

My mother didn't plan her sex talks. They just came up naturally as we spent time together. We would be working on something together in the kitchen, washing dishes perhaps, and one of us would bring up the subject of babies.

"Mommy, now where do the babies grow again?" we would ask.

"Well, there's a special pocket inside of you," she would reply, taking a Ziploc bag, filling it with water and sealing it, then talking about that "special pocket" in a woman. "It's in that bag of water that the baby gets to grow." Not where it *has* to grow, but where it *gets* to grow. She remained very positive and talked with such wonder and devotion about how precious it was to be a life-bearer that we loved hearing stories about pregnancy and childbirth. My dad—for a teen dad—was just as dynamic in his kitchen-table sex-ed instruction. He didn't just talk to me about shaving my legs; he was the one who showed me how to take the razor over my kness and around my shins.

81

Kids usually learn best with concise information presented in a few sentences, preferably with concrete, hands-on illustrations. That presents a challenge, especially when it comes to teaching kids about sexuality, but my mom and dad came up with creative illustrations from the materials at hand.

"Remember the period?" she added, as she took a cup and showed us how much blood would dribble out. There in the kitchen, while she washed dishes and I sat by the breakfast bar, she made the answers to our questions tangible.

Through conversations like this throughout my fifth- and sixth-grade years, she showed me a way of taking complicated material and breaking it down to its simplest components. I have passed on these skills to countless others in my parent-child seminars, teacher training sessions, and educational events for administrators and physicians. Today when I'm with someone at a restaurant, the swimming pool, a campfire—wherever—I'll grab whatever is handy to describe the reproductive system.

Kitchen-table sex ed uses common household items to illustrate what your kid is learning. For example, just about every book says the female human ovary is the size and shape of an almond. Get almonds in the shell to show your daughter what her ovaries look like. Seem funny? Pubescent kids seek answers from whomever is most accessible and whomever provides the information they're after *in a way they can understand*. This has the added side benefit of setting you up as the expert, the one who knows how to explain all these confusing realities. Your child will see that despite what she sometimes thinks, you really do know a thing or two about life.

When do you start kitchen-table sex ed? As we've stated before, it starts on the changing table. If you develop your presentation skills with a five-year-old—talking about how to wash hands, for instance—and do these sorts of things throughout your child's life, then later on when you talk about how to put in a tampon, your communication highway is clear and reliable. It's like connecting the dots: washing hands to washing the face to putting in a contact lens to putting in a tampon.

Kids will tell you when they want more information, not necessarily in words, but through body language. You help to add years to their emotional life by encouraging them, step by step. That's why we urge concerned parents to focus on their child's *emotional* age rather than their chronological age. Every kid is different, even within families. How does your child respond to your answers? That will provide a better indicator of how to discuss sexual development than your child's chronological age.

Hit the Road: Talking and Driving

"Mom, have you ever masturbated?"

It had been a normal drive. But at that point, the mother told me, "I tried to make sure my eyes didn't fall out of my head."

The daughter was most likely asking what to her seemed a normal question about a word she'd heard on television or in a conversation at school. She could have been asking a number of things, each with equal innocence. If the daughter did know what the word meant, her mom should consider it an even greater mark of trust that her daughter felt comfortable enough to bring it up with her. The beauty of such a question is that it is both a sign of trust and an open door for your response. You haven't worked hard for a decade at building your child's trust only to swat down such a question by saying, "We don't talk about things like that!"

A lot of questions come up as you drive. There's something very comforting about looking out the window and talking about life as the scenery passes by. Psychologists often tell people that if you want honest communication with your son or daughter, it must be eyeball-to-eyeball. Nothing could be further from the truth! Your son or daughter will find great comfort in looking out the window as they think, *I can't believe we're talking about this!* And yet your son or daughter, whether he or she is conscious of it or not, will be glad you're talking. This is so true that we *recommend* that if you're planning on talking about sex, you should consider taking your son or daughter for a drive. Riding in a car provides any number of natural distractions, which can help diffuse some of the natural uneasiness that comes from discussing such personal issues. If both parents can participate, so much the better; then you can laugh a little with each other and help diffuse the tension.

Tips for Talking

Consider a few tips for talking that we think will assist you in your assignment to begin practicing kitchen-table (or in-the-car) sex ed.

1. Always answer the question at an age-appropriate level. Learn to stall respectfully. "Mom, what are condoms and why are they flavored?"

Gabrielle and Jean had never discussed sex beyond talks about having a period, and Jean, the mother, felt mortified.

Unfortunately, she dealt with her discomfort by running off with far more information than necessary. "I ended up telling her everything about oral sex, things I'd never planned on telling her," Jean admitted. "I even went into great detail about the oral games some couples play." Finally, after an hour and a half, she reached the ragged conclusion of the lecture and told her daughter why condoms came in flavors. By that time, Gabrielle may have felt so overwhelmed with information that she no longer cared about the answer!

In our endeavor to be open, we sometimes give our kids more information than they want or need. This is why it's so important to know your kids individually, so that you can discern what they need and don't need.

A good technique is to respond to a question with another question: "Do you know what condoms are? Where did you hear about them?" This will give you a better idea of how specific your answer needs to be. With one ten-year-old you might think, *Okay, we can go there*, and get very specific. A different parent with a different ten-year-old may think, *My kid needs to mature a bit more before I discuss things like specific forms of birth control. For now, I'm simply going to say, "It's something married people use to prevent conception."*

One concern we have about the second approach is that some parents won't understand that their kid really could handle the answer, and so they won't ever talk about it. Or parents may think, *My kid would never want to know that,* when their kid is actually very curious. We forget that our kids live in a highly sexualized world.

Some answers, of course, are never appropriate. We know of one physician father who wanted his boys to know what women "really" look like, so he used a *Playboy* magazine as a way to show them "the real thing." It's sad that a grown man could equate pornography with "the real thing." This fantasized world is so unlike real life that his kids would have benefited much more from academic line drawings.

So just what *do* you do when your kids pop the questions? Your first agenda is to encourage this process so that they will feel they can ask again. When you're caught off guard, learn to stall respectfully. Many parents don't realize their kids know as much as they do, so some questions come as a shock; we've both met a number of well-intentioned parents who never dreamed their kids would ask such things. To prepare, mentally rehearse phrases such as:

- "That is a great question."
- "Is that what kids call it these days?"
- "What else did people say?"
- "Okay, let me see, where should I begin?"

If you don't feel comfortable answering on the spot, fine, but don't let the question slide. Make sure you get back to it, and make sure your kid knows you're going to get back to it. You could follow up with something like:

- "Give me some time to think how to answer that."
- "That's an interesting question. I will need to look that up; I want to make sure I answer it correctly."
- "Chances are, to really answer that question well, it will probably be later on tonight, maybe tomorrow, before I can get back to you. But I don't want you to think that I'm not going to answer that question, because I will."

Above all, take these questions in stride. Keep the communication highway open.

2. Practice. How do you learn to hit a curve ball? You practice. You anticipate its movement. You imagine that small, white sphere coming in and then picture yourself swinging your bat and hammering that ball right across the seams.

It's the same when talking with your kids about the changes of puberty. The time will come when the pitch sails your way, a nice, hanging curve ball just catching the corner of the plate, a real beauty.

And a strike against you if you let it go by.

We practice for all kinds of life's events: answering potential questions before a job interview, reading Scripture in front of the church, delivering lines for our role in the community play.

Silly as this may sound, you should also practice how you will respond to your kid's questions about sex. We don't mean memorizing canned responses. Think through your answers to questions you know your kids will have. What do you believe about masturbation? What reasons will you give your kids to wait for marriage to have sex? These two questions usually come up, and it's helpful to know your answers ahead of time. Even better, discuss your answers with your spouse to make sure both of you are on the same page. Practice may not make your presentation perfect, but it will help cut down on your awkward fumbling for words when the time comes.

3. Get feedback. If your kid doesn't understand what you've said, or if you provide an answer to something other than what he asked, true communication hasn't taken place. Sometimes getting feedback is easier *before* you answer the question. Sometimes it's helpful to repeat the statement in a different way to hear more from your kid. "You're asking me that because . . ." This usually gives your son an opportunity to state why he's asking the question and also lets him know that Mom and Dad are fine with talking about it. Also, you'll know if the response you have in mind will truly answer what he's asking.

If your son says, "Dad, I heard that someone can't get pregnant the first time they have sex," you could say something open-ended, something like, "Where did you hear that?"

"Well, Jimmy and I were on the playground, and that's what Brad said."

Your question helps keep an open door and communicates to your kid that you're open to talking back and forth and that you're taking it all in stride.

After you've finished with your answer, add an additional feedback question: "So, what do you think about that?"

He might say, "That makes sense," or he might add, "I'm not sure," and come up with a different question. We think it's a good idea for you to ask your child to respond to what you've just said so that you have an idea of what concepts actually got across.

4. Look at what families with older kids are dealing with. Discuss how you will deal with those same issues before you get there. The wise parent will recognize that an important part of kitchen-table sex ed goes beyond answering present questions to anticipating and discussing future issues.

A case in point from the Bell household: one year, the eighth-grade graduation party became the talk of the school. Our oldest child, John, was in seventh grade at the time, and part of him wanted to be nowhere else than in the limelight of popularity. He thrilled to gossip about the gathering that got out of hand. The host family's older siblings had spiked the punch, and the kids had played questionable music. The parents had taken a back seat at the festivities, retreating to the bedroom and allowing the kids full reign of the house. (Many parents of the invited kids had been falsely comforted, assuming that the parents would keep things under better control.) Kids thought that what had happened was funny; even some parents thought it was funny, though the boys' mother was appalled at what her sons had done. Unfortunately, this party became the talk of the school, and John craved being part of the in-crowd.

I couldn't let that moment pass. To have believed that no such event would ever occur again would have been crazy. I did not want to do battle a year down the road with my son, who was already bigger than me and growing ever more forceful in airing his opinions. The buzz about the party gave me the chance to talk with John about all the things he'd heard.

"First," I told him, "everything you've heard is a rumor. Some of it is probably true, and some of it is most likely not true. But you can't assume that *everything* you hear is true."

The party also gave us the chance to talk about what was coming up in the eighth grade and beyond: dances, parties, sporting events, even potentially staying overnight in hotels during the high school years when the football team traveled to other cities.

"You know Mom and Dad are going to have rules about all this," I told him.

"I know," he said.

At the time, I didn't even know what they were. I said, "We're going to have to think about how we do things," and I would joke with him, "because I know how important it is for you to be cool, right? At the same time you know that some of the things that happened at that party aren't going to fly in this family."

"Yeah, I know, Mom," he admitted.

Whenever Mike (my husband) and I were together for the remainder of that week, we talked about the rules we would set. Could John go to *any* party he was invited to? "No chance," Mike said.

"Well, you know we're going to drop him off and pick him up," Mike added. "At times, we're going to let someone else drop him off and pick him up if we trust that family."

I said, "When we get to a party, I want to be able to walk our kids in."

"That's going to be kind of awkward," Mike replied.

"Well, I've already told John that we will be asking some very specific things of him, and that's one of the things I'm going to say. I'm going to tell him that at this stage of the game"—I didn't give an age limit—"we're going to be walking him in."

During one of our lunch dates, I talked with John about our decisions and just laid things on the line.

"Look," I told him, "I know how important it is for you to fit in. Otherwise we wouldn't buy the kind of clothes that we buy, which are at least halfway up the scale of decency so that people won't make fun of you. I don't want to embarrass you by walking in with you. But I need you to count on the fact that I'm going to want to know what's going on. So if it mortifies you for us to walk you in, either don't ask to go to the party or just be aware of that ahead of time. I'm not going to hold your hand and walk you in like you're in kindergarten. I'll bring along a six-pack of soda or a bag of chips so it's not so awkward for you. I know how hard that's going to be for you, but I want to let you know that if you go in, I go in."

He rolled his eyes, but he felt okay with it because we weren't discussing it in the heat of the moment. It wasn't an emotional time; we hadn't just gotten in a fight. It occurred well ahead of the fact, *before* we had to consider a specific party.

Then we asked him, "What do you need from us?"

"Just don't smother me," he replied, and we let him talk to us about that concern. We all got very specific.

Finally, we told him, "John, find out the following information ahead of time or do not bother asking if you can go to the party":

- Will the parents be home and active in the party?
- Who will be in charge—the parents or the older siblings?
- What can you bring to help out with food?
- Will there be boys and girls at the party? What rooms in the house will be okay to be in, and what will the activities be?
- What kind of party is it? (We told him that if it was a "hang out" party, he could forget about going. Until kids have socialization skills, they should be focusing on an activity with parents involved.)

Since we wanted John to take responsibility as well, we told him that if anything questionable started happening, he should call us, and we would pick him up—no questions asked. If Mike and I had never met the host family, one of us would also phone the parents at some point before the party to introduce ourselves and ask a few questions, which might go something like this:

"Hi, Mrs. Jones, this is Kathy Bell. John is planning on coming to Zac's party this Friday night. I just wanted to double-check the directions on how to get to your house."

"——."

"Great. I also understand you and Mr. Jones will be home that night and quite involved in all the activities. If you think you need more help, I am available. I can flip hamburgers or whatever."

"——."

"Oh, you're having sub sandwiches—great. May I bring something when I drop John off?"

You get the idea. If I had sensed from my conversation that this seemed to be an inactive parent, John would have been warned ahead of time that this party was not a sure thing. Just because we headed out to a party did not mean we would stay. Yes, he felt mortified. But John also knows that his parents genuinely love him. He knows what is expected ahead of time.

A wonderful thing happened as a result of our conversations during this time. All year long, whenever John heard of a new scenario involving older kids, he brought it up at home and asked us how we would handle that situation when he got old enough to participate. This gave John and us plenty of time to prepare for his eighth-grade year and plenty of time to practice with smaller, more insignificant situations in his seventh-grade year. Because John knew the rules ahead of time, he began to decide on his own whether he would ask us about going. When he entered high school, he decided on his own that he wouldn't even ask about certain kinds of parties.

We were so proud when we'd ask him on some Friday or Saturday nights, "Why are you home?" and he would answer, "Because every party that's out there will be serving alcohol, so there's no way I'm going to go."

If you have a sixth grader, see what parents of seventh graders are dealing with. Next, talk with your sixth grader about how it will be next year. Those decisions and issues will come up, and it's better to talk about them before your child gets emotionally attached to a particular answer. Then when the pressure is on your child to fit in, he or she will already know the rules.

5. Help your children look past their limited experience to foresee potential problems. Here's a true story that should give every parent reason to pause.

Not long after thirteen-year-old Samantha moved into the neighborhood, Janice came by to meet the new kid on the block. Soon they were playing together, and Samantha felt pleased to fit in so quickly. As Janice left, she mentioned some other kids that she thought Samantha should meet, some "really cool guys" who lived around the corner.

Samantha's mother, who had a good relationship with her daughter, was smart enough to take note of the conversation, recognize the safety issues involved, and decide that initially her daughter wasn't going anywhere. "You know, sweetheart," she said later when they were alone, "there's no chance you're going to that house at this point. I don't know who these kids are or who their parents are."

Samantha and Janice continued to interact throughout the week, and with the weekend approaching, Janice asked, "Why don't you tell your mom that you're going to be at my house on Saturday night? The boys around the corner are having a party." It sounded like fun to Samantha, who rationalized that she could simply leave and walk home if she wanted.

But Samantha's mother recognized something fishy about her daughter's request, so she stepped in to say, "I'm sorry, Janice, she can't do it. Maybe another time." Janice left for the evening.

At ten o'clock that night, Janice's mother showed up at Samantha's house, asking if she knew where Janice was. She'd received a phone call, which was then cut off. Janice said she was at a party, that she was in trouble, and that she needed help. But the mother had no idea where she was. Samantha came out of the bedroom and said, "I think I know where she is. She talked to me about going to a party at some boys' house down the street."

Janice's mother figured out the place and called the police. Drugs and alcohol were flowing at the party, and Janice had been drinking, thinking it was cool and wanting to be a part of it.

Samantha had considered checking out the party because she saw it as no big deal. *If it's a dud,* she thought, *I'll just walk home. After all, it's just around the block.* The thought that she might not be *able* to leave did not cross her mind.

Kitchen-table sex ed assumes that we parents know more about potential problems than our kids do, with their limited experience. A young girl might not understand how things can get out of hand, and it's our job to explain how it might happen. This type of information is every bit as important as discussing bodily functions.

You know how dangerous it is to get in a car if the driver has been drinking, but do your kids? You know it's possible for decent kids to succumb to temptation when they spend long amounts of time alone, and it gets to be late, and they get a little tired, and their normal inhibitions get lowered. You know how forceful a young man can be when his passion gets out of hand, but does your daughter? She sees Billy as this nice, polite guy who cries during Hallmark commercials, but she's never seen Billy late at night, during a session of heavy petting, doing and saying things that would make him sick if he thought about it the next morning.

You're the parent. You have decades of experience, while your children are still idealistic and naïve. Use your experience to get involved and to look out for potential problems. Pay attention to that "uh oh" phenomenon, that little voice inside you that warns you something just doesn't smell right about a situation.

6. Be ready—with your facial expressions, with your eye contact, with your gestures, and with your body language—to answer anything. My (Kathy's) mother—Gloria Flores—promised to answer any question I had, and one day I came home and told her I had heard that unless a man was on top of a woman for at least three minutes, she would not get pregnant. I wanted to know if it was true. After all, Mom had said I could come to her anytime I wanted. I certainly took her at her word.

Your kids will most likely come to you with their questions when it's the last thing on your mind. You're never really expecting a conversation that goes something like:

"Mom, what's oral sex?"

"Well, Susie Q, it's funny you ask that, because I was just sitting here thinking about what oral sex is and how to talk about it with you."

Nah, it just isn't going to happen like that.

That afternoon I had caught my mom in a busy moment. She was looking for something in front of a dresser piled with papers. When I asked her my question, she just about fell over, and then she snapped at me that she didn't have time to answer that kind of a question. I took one look at her face and decided that I would never ask her a question about sex again.

Thankfully, I never carried out that decision, because I also remember her coming to me later and saying, "I blew that." She later offered me information, but for a while I was more cautious with my questions. You have to remember, she was still practically a kid herself. And she was also good at coming back humbly like a kid.

Expect the shock. Anticipate being surprised. Your kids will rarely choose the most opportune or appropriate moment to ask such questions.

One of the Leman daughters was only three when she threw me a humdinger of a curve. At the time, I was in the bathroom. Naturally, I had forgotten to lock the door, and in she walked. There I was, caught with my pants down, midstream.

"What's that?" she asked.

"That's Daddy's wristwatch," I replied hopefully.

"No, not your watch—that!" she said, pointing in the direction of a conversation I knew I was about to have.

"It's called a penis," I replied.

What do *you* say? Do you say it's Dad's tallywacker, his ying-yang, his wienie? Or do you say, "That's Daddy's penis"? Do you collect yourself to begin talking about the wonderful God-given gift of our sexuality? When that curveball comes, do you confidently take a swing, or do you back away from the plate and let it pass? Because if you freak out, you're already teaching your son or daughter something, and the lesson isn't a good one.

It's common for little girls to ask, "Do I have one of those? Does Mommy have one of those?"

No, she's not lucky enough to have one of these.

"No," you might respond, "you and your sisters and Mommy have vaginas, and your brother and Daddy have penises."

My saying "It's called a penis" seemed enough for her at the time. I didn't discuss the male and female reproductive system, how one day she would bleed from her vagina, and that when she was married, a man would put his penis in there. And I shouldn't have. That would have been way too much information for her age.

Now, do you think that when I went to take my morning leak, I expected my daughter to ask me about my penis? I had no way of knowing that my daughter would throw me that curve! People don't talk predictably about sex. Your kids aren't going to say things like, "Gee, Mom and Dad, that talk was great! Can you tell me more about how my penis works tomorrow morning while I eat my Frosted Flakes?"

You have no way of knowing that tonight your preschool-age daughter will come down to the living room, worried because she found a hole in herself "right here between my legs!" Or that tomorrow afternoon, when you're waiting in the grocery-store aisle, picking up the evening's dinner for guests, your son will ask why the woman on the magazine forgot to put her clothes on.

It's the same when kids reach the puberty years. To hit the curve, you should be ready to make the most of the opportunities when they come, and they will come.

Always remember: *Your reaction to every question is your kid's ticket to ask the next question.* Our bodies naturally reflect what is going on inside us. The first sign to your kids that they may be treading on eggshells is your facial expression and your body language. Your facial expression, your crossed arms, your tone of voice, your flustered air— all that will speak volumes to your pubescent child and have a major influence on whether he or she comes back for more. This is why an earnest heart is so important; you can't fake what's going on inside. In fact, your words are the last thing that will keep them coming back. The first thing they will remember when deciding whether to come back is your heart attitude.

7. Read. Get accurate information. One student informed my class that Mommy had told her that girls "bleed out all their eggs." That bothered me (Kathy), not only because I had to tell her in front of the class the correct information but also because my doing so made her realize that Mommy was wrong. That's a horrible place for a kid in front of her peers.

You owe it to your kids to give them accurate information. Read an anatomy book. Familiarize yourself with the proper terms. If you tell your kid something that makes his friends laugh at him, the chances of his coming back to you with another question aren't very good.

8. *Wrap it in the right context.* Always wrap conversations about sex in the right context—marriage.

"What's f***ing?" your daughter might ask after school one day, because she heard the word from her third-grade peers.

Do you respond by blowing up at your daughter and saying, "We *never* talk like that in this house!"?

Dad and Mom, your child doesn't even know what the word means. That's why she is asking about it. In fact, she's probably asking you because she feels out of place, assuming that the other kids know what it means. But the beauty of such a question is that it is asked in trust, and it gives you an opportunity to place your answer within the value system in which she's been brought up. She is saying, in essence, "This is what happened to me today, and I don't know what to make of it. How should I respond to this?"

"Oh, honey," you might say, without shaming her. "That's a terrible word for something beautiful that only married people should be doing. It's not a word you've ever heard Mommy or Daddy use, have you?"

See, now we're teaching kids about who we are. And you can take what could be simply a crass answer to her question and put a positive spin on it. "You know what that word really means? It's really talking about sexual intercourse."

"What's sexual intercourse?"

"Well, when you're married,"—you start right off by placing your conversation in the right context, marriage—"one of the neat things about becoming a couple is that you become one in many ways." And then you can explain about how God gave a daddy and mommy a wonderful way not only of making babies but of being close with their bodies. "You've heard people talk about sex. Let me tell you what sex is." You then talk about how Daddy puts his penis in Mommy's vagina, and that that's how babies are made. They're not found under a cabbage leaf, and a stork doesn't drop them down through the chimney. Take advantage of your child's question, even though it may seem premature.

My son, Kevin Leman II, heard the f-word when he was six, and I decided I was going to use the opportunity to tell him, in my own terms and with our family's value system, what God intends sex to be. He had already heard it expressed in filthy terms; now I wanted him to see it from another perspective. I want to wrap information about sex within the value system that I endorse. So I'm always going to reference marriage as I talk about intercourse.

Remember, this isn't a one-shot deal. You can't expect a six-year-old to fully understand what it means to have intercourse. There will be other opportunities. Pace yourself and take it in stride.

You can use these situations as teachable moments by saying, "You know, honey, I'm really sorry you heard that word, but you know what? You're going to hear people use terrible language and say things that are inappropriate all your life. You're going to have to make many decisions, just as Daddy and Mommy made decisions all our lives. Neither of us talks like that. Neither of us uses foul language."

The parents who freak out because they can't believe their son or daughter would even utter that word are the ones who lose valuable teaching moments. Kids today will shock you, as Kathy found out recently when a sixth-grade girl planted her foot on top of the desk in an exaggerated effort to show Kathy that she was always prepared. She unzipped a little pouch in her shoe and pulled out a condom she had stuffed in there, "just in case."

You may never dream of talking with your kid about condoms, because naturally *your* kid is never going to be involved with sex before marriage, right? Well, we have news for you. We live in a culture awash with sex, so even if your child never engages in sexual play, he will still get smacked in the face every day with the reality of a sex-saturated society: television, movies, magazines, lunchroom talk, locker pinups, and conversations among his peers.

If that sixth grader felt so eager to show her condom to Kathy, you can bet that more than a few classmates had seen it as well.

Instead of ignoring the condom machines at the local gas station's men's room—which you *know* your son has seen and has been curious about—bring up the topic on your own: "Hey, did you see what they're selling at the gas station? I want to spend some time talking to you about this."

Your kid's going to look at you and think, *Holy buckets—my parents are going to talk with me about* this?! But after you take this step, your kid will learn that he can talk with you about anything, because you brought up a topic he thought would never clear his lips, let alone his parents'. But if you don't talk with your kid about condoms and other things he will come across—or is coming across—he'll be left to guess at the relevant values that accompany them.

What we're talking about is removing the mystery for your child. Make sex and all its accoutrements seem like a wonderful and natural part of life—*within the marriage relationship*. Sex doesn't often get talked about that way today; if we don't make the value connection, no one will.

Wrapping your discussions in the context of your values also allows you to challenge faulty thinking. We live in a world with ads that trumpet condoms as the answer for everything. You may even want to pick up a box of condoms at the store and read it with your child: "Hmmm, it says these *reduce* the risk of pregnancy and disease, but it doesn't say they *eliminate* the risk. So what does that mean? Can we count on this? Will this take care of things 100 percent? Do you think maybe that's why it's best to save any kind of sex until marriage?"

Teachable moments will arise all the time as you listen to the radio or watch television or look through magazines. There are bus ads, newspapers, and even explicit advertisements in malls. More and more malls carry condoms in bathrooms, and this gives you a perfect opportunity for conversation.

"Oh, did you see that Planned Parenthood is putting condom machines in all the mall bathrooms?" you might point out. "Have you seen one yet? We sure never had anything like that in *our* bathrooms when I was growing up. Hey, the next time we're at the mall, remind me, because I'm going to go to the bathroom and buy one so we can talk about it."

You see, Planned Parenthood is eager to give out *information,* but that information usually gets presented in a value-free or even immoral context. Because they have millions of dollars at their disposal, they will get their advertisements in front of our children. That's a given. That's also why, as parents, we need to be clear about our expectations and to wrap such information in a value-oriented context: "Condoms can be helpful when you're married, because they allow you to choose, to a certain degree, when and how many children you want to have. But they're not 100 percent perfect; people get pregnant using condoms, and you know what? People can still catch diseases using condoms.

"I don't want you to have sex until you get married because I know you're a sensitive person and will have to deal with guilt if you rush things. I want your wedding night to be a very special night, perhaps the most wonderful night of your life. I don't want you to have to worry about a herpes outbreak just when you most want to celebrate your commitment to each other. I don't want you to enter into marriage already pregnant or with a child; I want you to be free to enjoy your spouse before you have children together. I want sex to be something you've waited on for a long time."

Your kids may roll their eyes, but in their hearts they'll be glad for the direction.

9. *Know your goal.* We just said you must know what you're talking about, and we've talked about creative ways that you can communicate that information.

Although providing accurate information so that you can be your child's primary educator *is* critical, you must never make that the primary goal. The real goal—more than communicating accurate information—is connecting with your child and demonstrating your concern. *Nothing else takes priority*. Excellent research and clear, accurate communication are all good, but if you never look at your kid to see what he or she is all about, then you're missing your child completely. Your genuine intimacy and attentiveness, on the other hand, will get embedded forever in your child's memory.

Let's go back to Samantha's story. Some parents, eager to be empty-nesters, might have gladly allowed Samantha to go out with Janice, even though something didn't seem right. Other parents might not take the time to give good, thorough answers to basic questions or to ask for feedback because it's almost 8:00 P.M. and they don't want to miss the first five minutes of their favorite sitcom.

How important are your kids to you, really? If your goal is to connect with your kids, you're going to have sacrifice other things. Kids aren't faucets that we can turn on and off at will. Sometimes they're open to discussing deep, personal issues; other times they have no interest in talking. Their hormones bring them through more moods in twelve hours than you go through in twelve days.

If you fail to walk through that door when it's open, there's no guarantee it will ever get opened again. Make it your goal to truly connect with your kids; don't see their questions as interruptions but as invitations to become more involved in their lives and to demonstrate your love for them.

A Part of Life

"I'm [sob] going to [sob] miss Rosie!"

The Leman family was headed to New York for Christmas, and our ten-year-old daughter, Lauren, had tears running down her face as she thought about saying good-bye to her dog for a couple of weeks.

"I know it's hard for you to say good-bye because you love your puppy," I told Lauren one night. "You're such a good mommy to Rosie, and you take such good care of her. You feed her, you're responsible—and you're only ten years old. How did I ever get so lucky to have a daughter like you?"

Lauren is a compassionate girl with a wonder for life. She loves to collect bugs from the yard in jars, and when she brings them into the house, we talk about how exciting it is that God made bugs' colors, shapes, and even abilities, so different. "It's the same with you and your sister," I often tell Lauren. "He's made you different from even your own sister."

That night as Lauren cried, I said, "I know you're going to miss Rosie; I'm going to miss Rosie, too. But we can be glad Rosie will be staying with a family that is responsible and that will take good care of her. And let's imagine what will happen when we come home from New York. What is Rosie going to do? She's going to run around, isn't she? She's going to jump all over and whimper that funny little sound she makes when she's so happy to see you."

Lauren nodded.

"Lauren, you know what?" I went on. "This is also a little preparation for what's coming. Just eight years from now, Daddy's probably going to take you away to college. I don't think it's going to be easy to say good-bye to each other, do you?"

"No."

"But you know what? You'll be able to come home for Thanksgiving, Christmas, and spring break."

This is what we mean by kitchen-table sex ed; you're sensitive to your child's development, and you relate everyday situations to life's larger context.

What does talking with Lauren about the dog have to do with sex? Doesn't seem like much, does it? And directly, it doesn't have much to do with sex. But indirectly, it has everything to do with sex. I'm filling her need for love by listening to her heart and affirming her as my daughter. I'm spending time with her; I'm not reading the newspaper at home or listening to the radio in the car when we're together. I'm involved; I'm answering her questions; I'm acting as her guide in this mysterious business called life.

And you know what? There's nothing else I'd rather do.

Chapter 7

First Base— Changes from the Neck Up

Teaching Your Child to Care for His or Her Face and Hair

"I HATE my face!"

The simple survey we took of eighth-grade students asked them to name their favorite female and favorite male celebrities and to state why they admired those two celebrities. Then we asked them to list the physical characteristics about themselves that they most appreciated.

The characteristics they most admired about their favorite celebrities were predictable—whatever hairstyle, nose shape, or exotic look was currently in fashion. When asked which characteristics they appreciated about themselves, the answers also seemed consistent.

"NOTHING!"

"I hate my weight!"

"I wish I were _____."

You fill in the blank.

Large letters and dark pencil marks emphasized their intense disgust. When *forced* to find something positive, the students chose innocuous characteristics.

"I think I have nice eyelashes."

"My feet are kind of cute."

"I'm not too short."

We noticed that the embarrassment students felt by fifth grade had blossomed into anger and shame by eighth grade.

"We can talk about anything else, but our bodies are disgusting," wrote one student. "I wish I was different, or someone else."

In a desperate attempt to measure up, students pour hours into primping, exercising, reading magazines, and working with their hair, all so that they can look like their favorite stars. When we told them how fashion photographers digitally retouch photos—changing models' clothes, smoothing wrinkles, enlarging breasts—the students' attitudes did not change: "At least Jennifer Love Hewitt was born with something to work with. I wasn't."

I can recall that as a young girl, I, too, looked in the mirror and nearly passed out with fright. When I was three, a car accident knocked out my two front teeth, leaving a gaping hole for the longest time. When my teeth finally came in, they were so huge that kids called me "Beaver." They also teased me about my naturally curly hair. To stop kids from calling me a poodle, I even wore a swim cap to bed one night to see if that would straighten my hair.

It didn't.

I was fat, big-haired, and beaver-toothed. How's that for a fifth-grade photo? I felt I was less attractive than a dirty piece of gum on the bottom of a tennis shoe, and eventually I used food to help numb my pain. Finally, one day I looked in the mirror and came to a conclusion: "Well, I guess this is it," I admitted. "Either I learn to appreciate this—or what else is there? I have no choice but to do the best I can with what I have."

So began my own journey of acceptance, the same journey I help kids make today. The journey begins with helping our children understand what is going on in their bodies during pubescence.

The Coordinator: The Pituitary Gland

The grand coordinator of our children's changing bodies is their pituitary gland, which functions something like a wedding coordinator. Weddings are celebrations on the grandest scale. They represent times of laughter, joy, and festivity. They also involve an inordinate amount of work.

Take the royal and celebrity weddings of the twentieth century, for example. Imagine having to coordinate the thousands of man-hours put in by florists, bakers, caterers, seamstresses, interior designers, and TV and radio production crews. Think of arranging St. George's Chapel with thousands upon thousands of roses, lilies, stephanotis, and, to quote the florist, "all the delphiniums in the country" to match the flowers in the bouquet Sophie carried down the aisle for her wedding to Prince Edward. [1] Somebody had to choose those flowers, pick them, transport them, and then arrange them! Or imagine handling $100,000 worth of security for Brad Pitt and Jennifer Aniston's wedding—a potential paparazzi feeding frenzy—which involved the Federal Aviation Administration and the hiring of a Los Angeles Police Department helicopter to control the swarm of helicopters buzzing over the wedding. (The job of coordinating it all fell to a former Israeli secret service agent.[2]) Prince Charles and Diana Spencer's wedding, often called the wedding of the century, involved untold efforts simply to broadcast it on television to the approximately 750 million people who tuned in.[3] And imagine meticulously sewing 10,000 mother-of-pearl sequins onto Diana's dress, which required so much material that plans to design it from British silk had to be changed because all the silkworms in England could not meet the demand.[4]

The details are enough to give anyone a headache; now imagine coordinating them all, being the one person responsible for making sure *everything* is ready for the big day.

The tiny pituitary gland, the size of a frozen pea but shaped like a kidney bean, is the body's master gland behind the changes of puberty and the coordinator of the developing child's growth. Physically speaking, puberty begins when the brain stimulates the pituitary gland to secrete hormones; these hormones in turn stimulate our organs' growth. Fluctuations in our emotions result from the chemical hormone messages our bodies receive: estrogen and progesterone for females, and testosterone for males. The body is readying itself for adulthood and preparing its systems for reproduction.

You can observe the effects of these hormones years before any of the more noticeable physical changes occur. If you were to track your child's emotions on a calendar—up days and down days—you would

---

Pituitary Gland: A Practical Kitchen-Table Sex-Ed Lesson

Materials needed: One dry, red kidney bean; one frozen dinner pea; and one large cauliflower.

Objective: To understand the size, shape, and location of the pituitary gland, responsible for the child's growth.

Frozen pea: Represents the size of the pituitary gland.

Kidney bean: Represents the shape of the pituitary gland.

Cauliflower: Cut in half lengthwise, represents the two halves of the brain; the pituitary gland would be located between these halves, roughly at the base of the florets.

begin to notice a pattern indicating whether your child had a cycle of twenty-one days, or thirty-six days, or something in between.

Hormones will tell a child's hair to straighten, curl, thicken, thin, frizz, even change color. While genetics plays a primary role in all this, hormones add to the commotion that inevitably spells bad-hair days, and dreaded voice changes for pubescent boys and girls. And then, of course, there are the changes in skin and all the problems that acne brings. Genetics may dictate whether kids need glasses for their eyes and braces for their teeth, but hormones intensify how kids perceive themselves throughout these changes.

It would be one thing if all this were pulled off with a smooth, fluid motion; unfortunately, it more closely resembles the starting and stopping, speeding up and slowing down, of rush-hour traffic.

Going back to our royal and celebrity wedding analogy, a good coordinator knows that things don't always go as planned. As a case in point, imagine having to call a jeweler for an emergency repair on the band of Elizabeth's tiara just as she prepared to head off in her gold, horse-drawn coach.[5] Or having only five days to recreate the wedding dress for Jacqueline Onassis after a flood ruined the dress you'd been working on for two months.[6]

Unexpected "mishaps" take place in our children's pubescent bodies every single day. Nothing seems to go as planned. Your child's body is changing into something completely different, and the herky-jerky experience can feel both exciting and frightening. Hair and skin represent the two biggest challenges for most young kids, so let's deal with each in turn.

Bad-Hair Days

"Mom, I need a new haircut," a daughter says.

"Your hair looks fine," her mother tells her.

"But do you know how long it took me to get it to stay like this?" her daughter asks. "It doesn't stay straight like it used to."

The wise mother will take her daughter's concerns seriously. Hairdressers can tell you that most parents do not understand their child's legitimate need to try different shampoos and new hairstyles. Most parents hear this request to get a new 'do as a desire to look more mature or cool. But more likely, the request is based on physical changes in your daughter's body. Her hormones are creating new problems with the hair follicles and thus with her hairstyle. Pubescent kids have many bad-hair days.

Frequent grooming requests from your child are normal and understandable at this age. If we help guide this behavior instead of dismissing it out of hand, we set up our kids for success. During the early years of your child's puberty, focus on a few things from the neck up that seem reasonable and age-appropriate: hair care, proper oral hygiene, skin care, and sunscreen use.

A good haircut can make the difference in how well your child can manage her hair. If she wants her hair to look a certain way, bring a picture of that hairstyle and ask the stylist if her hair can be cut and styled that way. It may, and it may not. The goal is to work with what she has and with what her body is changing into.

Face Shapes and Hairstyles (for Girls)

Different hairstyles are best suited to different face shapes. To determine the shape of your face and complementing hairstyles, two measurements are necessary:

Width: measure from the center of one earlobe to the center of the other earlobe.

Length: measure from the hairline to the bottom of the chin.

Round length and width measurements to the nearest quarter of an inch (1/4" = .25), and divide the length by the width (length/width) to get the decimal number indicating your face type.

Face Shape	Range	Average
Oblong	1.2–1.3	1.25
Heart	1.3–1.37	1.34
Diamond	1.371–1.41	1.39
Oval	1.411–1.45	1.43
Round	1.451–1.458	1.47
Square	1.481–1.52	1.5
Triangle	1.521–1.69	1.6

Oblong: Your face is long and thin, with a generally uniform width from top to bottom (but more rounded than the square face) and often with a pointed chin. (A Disney character with an oblong face shape is Mulan.)

Try: Short to medium styles (middle-of-the-neck length is best) with volume in curly, wavy, or layered styles at the sides of your face to add width and balance to your long, slender face. You also may be able to wear straight-back styles.

Avoid: Styles that are too high at the crown or too long (don't wear past shoulders), as these will appear to lengthen your face.

Heart: Your face is wide at the forehead and narrow at the chin (e.g., Disney's Belle in *Beauty and the Beast*).

Try: Chin-length or longer styles, which suit you best. Those with dramatic heart-shape faces wearing shorter styles should balance their wonderful cheekbones with volume behind the neck.

Avoid: Short styles that are full on the crown, which add too much weight to the upper face and make you look top-heavy. Also avoid slicked-back styles.

Diamond: Your face features high, wide cheekbones, and narrows at both the forehead and jaw line (e.g., Disney's Aurora in *Sleeping Beauty*).

Try: True diamonds (balanced at forehead and chin) can try almost any style. Those with dramatic diamond-shape faces (accentuated angles) should balance their cheekbones with volume behind the neck.

Avoid: As long as you don't cover your face (show your wonderful features!), just about anything is fair game.

Oval: Your face is slightly more narrow at the jawline than at the forehead, with gentle rounded curves (e.g., Disney's Princess Jasmine in *Aladdin*.)

Try: Short, medium, or long—almost any hairstyle looks good on you because of your balanced features. Style hair off your face to show your facial features. (Slicked-back styles work as well.)

Avoid: Covering your face with your hairstyle; let your beautiful facial features show!

Round: Your face appears full—wide at the cheeks with a round jawline and hairline (e.g., Disney's Boo in *Monster's, Inc.*)

Try: Styles with height at the crown (layering the top may help). Style hair close at the sides so that your face appears longer and more narrow.

Avoid: Rounded and straight-back styles. Short, cropped hair that does not show from the front does not complement your face.

Square: Your face features a strong square jawline, typically matched by an equally strong hairline (e.g., Disney's Tinker Bell in *Peter Pan*).

Try: Short to medium-length styles (a bit below the chin to shoulder-length is best) with volume moving forward onto the face. Consider curls or wave to give your hair body and to soften your face's angles.

Avoid: Long, straight styles that emphasize the straight lines of your jaw and forehead.

Triangle: Your face is narrow at the forehead and widens at the jawline—the reverse of the heart-shape face (e.g., Disney's Meg in *Hercules*).

Try: Short styles with fullness at the temples. Style hair off the face to show more width at the forehead (taper hair over the ears and along the cheeks toward the jaw, or tuck hair behind ears).

Avoid: Extra fullness at the jawline, as this accentuates the lower part of your face.

When it comes to hair-care products, applying more is not better, and not knowing the simplest hair-care skills can cause problems.

"My son has a scalp problem," some parents say, "and we're not sure what it is."

We've found that many boys not only use way too much shampoo, they don't completely rinse it out of their hair. They dump on about a cup of shampoo, swish it around in their hair, then dump on another cup of conditioner, and then swish that around without rinsing thoroughly. Then they put in gel after the shower.

"Show me how much shampoo you use in the shower," we ask boys in our hygiene classes.

Kids pour a handful.

"No wonder!" parents say. "*That's* where my money's going!"

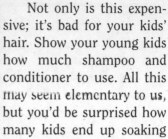

Hair Tip

For the hair's health, rotate your child's brand of shampoo and conditioner at least every other month.

Not only is this expensive; it's bad for your kids' hair. Show your young kids how much shampoo and conditioner to use. All this may seem elementary to us, but you'd be surprised how many kids end up soaking their heads in these products. Tell your kids to start out with an amount the size of a dime. If your kid has long or thick hair, move up to a nickel size—but never more than a quarter size. Make sure you tell them to use their fingertips to massage it in, and to completely rinse it out of their hair.

If they have short hair, they may not need conditioner at all. If they have long hair, they should apply conditioner at the midway point of the hair shaft, near the neck, and move down toward the ends of the hair. Natural oils will replenish the hair shaft near the scalp.

Hair Type

"I want you all to go down the aisle and choose a shampoo for your hair."

After first working with the girls to determine their hair types, my (Kathy's) hygiene consultant, Melissa, took them to the grocery store to see what shampoos they would choose. The girls buzzed off down the aisle and spent time poring over the 100-plus different hair-care items before bringing back their choices. Melissa needed only one look at the girls and the shampoos each had chosen.

Every single girl chose a shampoo based on what fragrance she liked. Not one had the correct shampoo for her hair type.

Like those girls, many of us still choose shampoos for their scent or brand name, without considering how it will affect our hair. Then we wonder why our hair feels brittle, lifeless, greasy, or just plain gnarly! Figuring out the hair type for your child is quite easy.

What's Your Hair Type?

1. Pick a weekend.
2. Wash your hair Friday morning, without applying conditioner.

3. Wait two days without washing to see what type of hair you have:
   - If within six hours your hair looks dull and as if it hasn't been washed, you have "oily" hair.
   - If your hair still looks clean by the next day, you have "normal" hair.
   - If you have dry, flyaway hair by the end of the second day, you have "dry" hair.

Pretty easy, huh? And if your kid does it over a weekend, it's no big deal.

Once you know whether your kid has oily, normal, or dry hair, the next time you go to the store looking for shampoo, make sure you read the label. Does it match your kid's hair type? Now, before you throw that big bottle into your cart, buy a trial-size bottle or the smallest size available to test it out first. Just because the bottle says "oily" doesn't mean it's going to work well with your kid's hair. That way you'll end up saving money by avoiding wasted product.

The End of the World: Mount-Everest Pimples and Skin Care

Ask a classroom of kids which facial care products they'd choose, and you're likely to get thirty different answers—few of them based on what their faces actually need. Again, most kids base their decisions on brand reputation, on fragrance, or on what is currently being marketed by the latest Hollywood movie star. But what your kid needs to realize is that her body, not Elizabeth Hurley's, calls the shots.

"Hi, are you Kathy Bell?" a woman asked me at Starbucks.

"Yes," I replied.

"We attended your hygiene class, and I just wanted to let you know about the change in my son."

"Tell me about it."

She had argued with her fifth-grade boy about washing his face, combing his hair, and brushing his teeth. But when we told him that his body was in charge, that he needed to choose hair- and skin-care products according to his particular body chemistry, he finally got the message and started taking care of himself. Because guess what? The hair and skin will tell you whether they like what you put on them, and when they say no, you have no choice but to stop and listen. Nobody wants pimples or bad-hair days.

If you break it down this simply, kids think, *Wow, my face really is in charge. Mom and Dad are right.* They start listening to both you and their bodies. Before you were telling him, "Wash your face." Now he has a routine to follow: rinse face with warm water, rub cleanser gently in a circular motion (don't scrub), splash with cold water, clean ears with washcloth when cleaning face, pat face dry, and apply sunscreen in the morning. Once it becomes familiar, the entire process will take only a few minutes.

"Do you know that we no longer have any problems with this, Kathy?" the mom said.

Why is skin care so important? It yields enormous, long-term effects. You've heard the fable of the ants and the grasshopper, haven't you? The ants work hard at storing food throughout the year while the grasshopper sings and dances the days away, enjoying himself without a care. When winter comes, guess who arrives begging at the ants' home, humbly knocking on the door because he has nothing to eat?

Skin care is like that. Childhood is the spring of our skin's life. If we didn't know better, it would seem our baby-faced complexion could forever bounce back from the bite of sun and wind. But eventually age and weather bring wrinkles, and skin grows tired. The winter of our later years arrives, and if we haven't made proper skin care a daily, lifelong pattern, we can wind up with serious dermatological problems.

Sunscreen is probably the most important skin-care item a child can use. If this one item does not get used consistently, your kid is not ready

---

Testing Skin-Care Products

1. Because different people have different pH balances, first buy a trial-size product (if available) to test if it is compatible with your child's body chemistry.
2. While at home, have your child put a bit of the product on the underside of the forearm (better to have a reaction there than on the face).
3. Any adverse reactions will usually occur soon after application, but leave the lotion or cream on for a full twenty-four hours to see whether a rash or a red spot develops (signs of an allergic reaction).

to move on to other skin-care products. Most doctors recommend an SPF (sun protection factor) of thirty or higher. If your child is fair-skinned and burns easily, be advised that early-childhood sunburns may lead to an increased probability of skin cancer later in life.

Some skin areas are best left alone. The facial skin tissue around the eyes is particularly delicate; unfortunately, that is just the place every teenage girl loves to apply the latest eye makeup. Have your daughter spend the next week looking at women's sagging, bagging eyes, and ask her if that is what she wants.

The truth is, most kids tend to focus more on immediate skin problems, especially acne. During puberty, hormonal surges stimulate the production of sebum, or oil, in the skin. Normally this passes through pores to the skin's surface, but sometimes the channel gets blocked, creating the infamous "third eye." In westernized societies, acne is a nearly universal skin disease, afflicting 79 to 95 percent of the adolescent population.[7] Maintaining a healthy lifestyle and washing the face to remove extra oils can help to alleviate acne.

If your child has severe acne, genetics are the most likely cause. Unfortunately, while frequent washing and the latest zit cream can help, they won't get rid of severe acne. Nor will swearing at your parents or ancestors! Seeing a dermatologist will provide some relief, as can a trip to the local health-food store for natural remedies.

What else can you do?

- Teach your children to keep their hands away from their face.
- Frequently clean any items that come into contact with the face, such as the phone receiver, and towels. Change pillowcases often.
- Although washing one's face is a good habit, doing it more frequently or vigorously will not help acne go away. Acne is genetic. If it runs in your family, you may need to take your child to a physician.

Take Products for a Test Drive

Your skin is a sensitive organ. It responds to searing summer days by opening the pores and to bitter winter cold by closing them. But temperature is just one of many influences that affect the skin. Our skin will also react to all the soaps, conditioners, lotions, creams, perfumes, and deodorants that we apply and even to the chemicals left on our clothing from laundry detergent.

Facial Skin Care

Facial skin needs to be kept clean and moisturized.

1. Open pores by splashing warm water on face.
2. Use a skin cleanser without deodorizers or antibacterial chemicals, following the directions on the package, and massage product into face (do not scrub).
3. Splash cool water on face to rinse and close pores.
4. Pat face dry; don't wipe face vigorously.
5. Finish with sunscreen (nonoily) and lip balm to protect and moisturize.

Listening to your skin means slowing down enough to test one product over a twenty-four-hour period. You can tell your kids, "I want to make sure you're not going to break out with this stuff." Your kid feels thrilled because you spend time with him on his face—for which he has a passionate concern. Buy the trial-size bottle and bring it home for a test drive. Did he get a rash? Did her skin burn? Did it turn red?

When we test skin-care products with kids in the classroom, invariably at least one kid will develop a small rash from a product.

"Here's what it looks like," our hygienist, Melissa Scott-Pozarowski,[8] will say. "Here's what can happen. This is why it's important to listen to your skin."

As kids show maturing characters, they can move on to other products such as makeup. But they first need to show responsibility with the basic skills, demonstrating proper use of personal-care products so that they don't ruin their skin, and proving they can organize the products in the bathroom—in a drawer, under the sink, or perhaps in Kleenex boxes with the lids cut off.

Fashion Statements

Neck-up issues inevitably go beyond skin and hair to include piercings. Culturally, a lot of kids have their ears pierced as infants. Ten-year-old Lauren Leman recently worked up enough courage to have her ears pierced, and fifteen-year-old Hannah's ears are pierced at the lobe and then once more above the lobe. Now, if she comes to me and says she's going to have her tongue or her navel pierced, I'm going to say no. How did Sande and I decide all this? As our daughter's parents, we made a judgment call. They may not be right for the family next door, but they're right for our family.

We're very particular, especially at this stage of Hannah's life, about what battles we want to fight. Frankly, if Hannah said she wanted to put tin cans on her ears, God bless her. She'll walk a little lopsided, and a lot of her friends may even think it's cool, but I'll bet that the weight of those cans will get to her until she goes back to something halfway normal.

I remember when our son, Kevin, was in his teens and announced that he wondered about getting his ears pierced. I didn't react—which he noticed—choosing instead to bide my time. The next day I came to the dinner table with one of Sande's earrings clipped onto my earlobes.

"Dad," Kevin said, "you look absolutely ridiculous!"

"Really?" I said. "Your mom likes it!"

Without saying a word to Kevin, and without him saying a word to me, the message got across. Kevin's earlobes remain unpierced to this day.

Don't underestimate the power of humor during this embarrassing period of your child's life. If you notice she has a third eye coming out of her forehead, talk and laugh about the biggest zit you ever had. If you need to talk to your child about bad breath, use an example from your own life about how you once killed a horse by blowing in its face.

The key is to put this trying time of your kid's life into perspective: it's here, everyone has gone through it, and it'll pass. That tangly hair will eventually get thinner; the acne will take a vacation; the pituitary gland will eventually slow things down. The important thing is that you're there as the moderating influence: sometimes funny, always empathetic, always taking the time to stay involved in this very important season in your child's life.

Oral Hygiene

Your child will begin to notice that he occasionally has bad breath.

- Brush teeth, floss, and use mouthwash daily. Schedule regular dental checkups.
- When brushing teeth, use an amount of toothpaste about the size of a pea. Brush the tongue also to help prevent bad breath.

Chapter 8

Second Base—Changes from the Neck to the Waist

Teaching Your Child to Deal with Overall Body Changes

Early one evening my daughter Amy (Bell) was heading out the door to go to the homecoming football game with a group of friends. Like most high school girls, Amy's friends wore shirts with plunging necklines and jeans that leave a hint of midriff. Amy herself wore a low-cut purple shirt that just hit the top of her jeans. But what caught my attention—and would have caught the attention of every high school boy whose testosterone exceeded his self-control—was that its see-through fabric gave a tantalizing glimpse of her bra.

"Amy," I said, "I can see your bra."

"Yeah," she admitted. "This shirt is a little small, too, isn't it?"

"Amy," I replied, "you're not going anywhere in that shirt."

As girls move into the later puberty years, Dad's opinion begins to matter more, especially when it comes to areas such as appropriate fashion. Because Amy will occasionally butt heads with me, whereas she won't with her father, I found Mike and said, "You might want to take a look at that shirt Amy's got on."

It took only half a look. "Amy, that shirt looks like it's a little too small," Mike said. "Are you *sure* you didn't put your little sister's shirt on?"

"I'm sure."

"Where'd you get it, anyway?"

"It's not mine. It's Suzanne's."

"Okay, then why don't you give it back to Suzanne? Because it's not going out the door on your body, babe," he said.

"Oh, Dad."

"Nope. Grab something else, because you're not wearing that shirt."

As long as there are parents and kids, there will be clashes over what is acceptable. That's true in the Bell house, it's true in the Leman house, and we're sure it's occasionally true in your house, as well. Teaching your kids about appropriate dress is part of every parent's job description. After all, they don't know what's best for them; they're kids!

"What is it about those kinds of clothing?" one friend asked. Every one of Amy's friends waiting for her in the car sported a shirt with a plunging neckline, cut right above the jeans so that you could see the stomach. "She already wants to show off the hardware," said another parent of her fifth-grade daughter who wanted to wear a bikini, not to swim in, but to walk around the pool.

Hiding the Hardware

Middle school girls often get a shock when we explain that most guys prefer women who dress modestly. Subtlety is alluring in a way that brazenness just isn't. That's why males consider the woman who doesn't show it all much more sexy than a woman who completely reveals her God-given beauty. Men have always been—and always will be—attracted by mystery. If you show everything you've got, there's nothing to look forward to!

Tell *that* to your daughter whose hormones need direction.

Oh, there are always those few boys who seem entranced by immodestly dressed girls, but those aren't the types of boys your daughter wants to attract. Both of us are old enough to remember an old *Happy Days* episode when Joanie Cunningham slipped out of the house, dressed to kill and made up like a vamp. She got into a dangerous situation with some boys but got saved just in time by the Fonz, who took Joanie aside and warned her, "Joanie, just remember: when you put out an ad, someone might answer that ad."

Discussing modesty with your kids is not just "a talk"; it's a way of life. It begins with demonstrating modesty by how *you* dress. If you want to teach modesty, you'd better be modest yourself. My wife is always telling me to put on my clothes, because my natural tendency is to walk around in my shorts.

"Leemie," she'll say to me, "would you put your clothes on?"

"Why?" I ignorantly reply.

"Because you have four daughters, that's why."

Good point.

Modesty goes beyond modeling appropriate dress to include talking about photographs you see in ads, in *People* magazine at the doctor's office, or on one of those award shows on TV. If an actress is wearing a see-through dress that censors have to partially blur out because they can't air it over the network, talk with your kids about the values behind such a choice.

Some parents want their kid to fit in so badly that they won't impose any constraints on his or her dress, but do you really want your kid to be like everyone else? If so, get ready for an out-of-wedlock pregnancy, drug use, and considerable emotional trauma, all before your child reaches the age of twenty-one.

Fortunately, God has already built in a tendency toward modesty that we can work from, as long as it hasn't been destroyed. I (Kathy) recognize this in my girls' development classes when I show a slide depicting the female crotch; the collective embarrassment gets so thick it's almost like a curtain.

"I know this is probably embarrassing," I say, "and your first thought may be, *I don't want to look at this or talk about this*. But understand that the feeling you have right now is a good one. It's called modesty, and it is that feeling that tells you this is something private, something not normally discussed with other people in the room. I do not want you to let go of that feeling; I want you to hold on to it. It helps protect you when you cross boundaries. No one should tell you that feeling should go away. If you get that feeling when someone is touching you, that's the uh-oh feeling that you need to pay attention to; it's telling you to get out of there."

I describe that feeling to kids as a sixth sense that protects them from trouble. When kids become sexually active, allowing others to move freely across boundaries into their private spaces—emotional or physical—they begin destroying God's incredible gift of intuition that alerts them to things not right. If your daughter allows boys to do this, convincing herself that what she's doing is okay, she rewrites those protective mental messages. She needs to protect herself against this erosion, because if she lets her natural sense of modesty diminish, she'll have a long and difficult journey to get it back.

Parents, you, too, should respect this sixth sense of your child. If your daughter's fifth-grade class is preparing to study reproduction and she says emphatically, "I'm *not* ready for this," and her response seems something more than just I-don't-want-to-go-to-school avoidance, you should honor her feeling about this. When you respect your child's development, she will learn a far better lesson than if you push her to get in step with the rest of class that particular week. Anyway, reproduction is something you can cover at home.

Besides, many schools today have an almost criminally cavalier disregard for modesty. One spring I (Kathy) was asked to observe a speaker talking to middle school boys about puberty. Some of the boys played with pencils or the gum under the chairs. Others seemed genuinely interested as the speaker described and discussed the changes of puberty. A few boys acted like—well, like Dr. Leman acted in middle school!—trying to be the center of attention, causing trouble, cracking jokes, that kind of thing. There were only a handful of boys acting this way, but they *were* a handful.

The interest in the room quickly escalated to a fevered pitch when the speaker began fielding questions about sexual activity and, specifically, about what happens to a woman's body when she is aroused. The class reacted to the instructor's answers in a typical way. The boys not yet ready for this information looked aghast. The boys who showed genuine interest giggled uncomfortably. But some of the boys asking the questions nearly jumped out of their seats with excitement as their questions grew ever more specific.

I left that school with a knot in my stomach. If I were the parent of one of those kids, I would have been furious. I wondered what those boys would do with all their sexually charged energy. I knew from experience that many of them would use their newly acquired information to unmercifully tease their female classmates.

Boys need to learn modesty, too. Particularly, when a guy makes fun of the girl sitting next to him in English class, he needs to understand that she will already be through the changes of puberty when he's in the thick of it: that scrubby half beard, the suddenly squeaking voice. His turn is coming! His best bet is to keep his mouth shut.

With some girls, we have to help them overcome a *false* modesty. In my mother-daughter classes, I (Kathy) tell the girls, "Part of your homework is that I want you to take a mirror and see what your body looks like down at your private parts, your vaginal area."

The girls gasp, mortified.

"You don't have to do it today," I add. "I simply want you to know what things look like when it's healthy. If you get a rash down there from bubble bath, I want you to be able to recognize that things look different.

I also want you to know where the tampon goes. If you're on swim team and you start your period, you cannot wear a pad in the pool. How many of you want to talk with the coach about putting in a tampon? I'm simply asking you to look now so that you know where a tampon goes in case you have to do something quickly."

By knowing and respecting their bodies, kids will nurture their precious sixth sense.

Measuring Up

"Daddy," my daughter, Lauren, told me one day, "I'm so glad I'm a girl."

"Why's that?" I asked.

"Oh," she replied, "I just think it's easier to be good when you're a girl."

Funny as that sounds, there is truth to it. Boys do all sorts of weird things, such as peeing out of second-story windows to see whose stream can stretch the farthest. When it comes to maturity, pubescent girls seem to have a jump on boys on many levels.

What is maturity? One of my (Dr. Leman's) favorite discussions comes from the TV show *Everybody Loves Raymond*. One night Raymond had a guys' night out with his buddies, and they did the same stupid things they always used to do when they were out: spitting ice cubes, hassling waitresses, telling corny jokes, and doing other juvenile things you might do in seventh or eighth grade. Raymond came home depressed and told his wife that he didn't have a good time doing the same childish things he used to enjoy so much.

"Raymond," his wife said, "I've waited for this moment for years." *Dramatic pause.* "You're growing up!"

People don't really grow up until they're about twenty-one. If you think that's off-the-wall, call any auto insurance agent and talk about insurance rates. When you're twenty-one years old, you may think, *I'm legal!* But if you ask anyone who just turned twenty-one if they feel grown up, 99 percent of them will tell you, "Well, no, actually I don't." It takes time, and people want instant maturity. You must wait until you are sixteen to drive, eighteen to vote, twenty-one to drink, and twenty-five to benefit from a drop in insurance rates. There's a reason we don't let anyone under thirty-five run for president of the United States: maturity.

Everyone matures physically, emotionally, and spiritually at different rates. If you have a thirteen-year-old girl with a seemingly eighteen-year-old body, that has potential trouble written all over it, because the sixteen- or seventeen-year-old boy doesn't see her thirteen-year-old personality; he's mesmerized by that eighteen-year-old body! A thirteen-year-old girl with breasts is not inherently more mature than a thirteen-year-old girl without breasts; physical development does not correlate to emotional development. Her immaturity and naïveté can get her into all kinds of predicaments, so make sure you keep early developers within the same social strata as their peer group, because the difference between a sixteen-year-old and a thirteen-year-old is not three years; it's eons. Don't make the mistake of thinking, *Well, because she's mature for her age, she can handle it*. That line of thinking encourages your child to grow up too quickly and pushes her into circles she doesn't belong in. You don't let your ten- or twelve-year-old daughter bum around with fifteen-year-old boys. "'If I had a daughter who had a period at nine,' says Dr. Mary Pipher, 'I'd say, "This does not mean you're a woman; it means you're a nine-year-old having a period, and we are going to proceed accordingly."' That means clothing, books, and music appropriate to a girl's chronological age.... It also means having her hang out with her family, where peer pressure to act sophisticated isn't a problem."[1] Your daughter's girlfriends may look like kids next to an adult woman, but gauge your daughter who has bloomed early by her *emotional* age, not by her physical development.

As with all situations, talk about it. You could say, "Honey, you've been blessed with some physical features that are really nice. As you can tell by looking around at your classmates, you're the only one in your class like this. With that comes a burden, because people are going to see you as older. You're going to have to remember that you're just like your friends who are also eleven or twelve years old." Keep your child treading water; don't allow her to enter circles beyond her emotional reach.

Late bloomers have a different set of challenges. In New York, where I grew up, they separated the boys from the girls during our school's swim class and made us swim in the nude—and I mean as naked as the moment we came into the world. I remember standing for roll call, heels on the edge of the pool in alphabetical order, and looking over at the guy next to me. He was a *man!* There I was, a boy with a voice still fit for boys' choir! *When am I going to grow up?* I remember thinking. *When am I going to have pubic hair? When am I going to look like a man? When am I going to have hair under my armpits?*

Dads, do you remember looking for that first little hair, then rejoicing when it came in? It's like a trophy.

Late bloomers need to know that their time will come. They may be struggling with insecurity as they look at their peers—the girls wondering if they will ever develop breasts, the boys wondering if they will ever exceed five feet in height or hear their voice drop in pitch. As always, helping your son or daughter through this time by affirming their masculinity or femininity will help fill the void that may now seem to them especially deep and wide.

Dealing with the Hand They've Been Dealt

When he was in late puberty, Kathy's husband, Mike, would measure his height against one particular brick in the school hallway as he walked by. He also watched others as they passed the same brick for comparison, especially girls in whom he had an interest. He wanted to be sure they weren't taller than he was if he was going to spend any time with them.

When it comes to the changes of puberty, it doesn't do any good to tell kids what they already know—that everybody, for example, grows to be a different height. Kids already know that. What they want to know is how to live with the hand they've been dealt. How do we teach this?

We have an exercise we like to encourage our clients and their children to participate in every now and then. "Go to the local mall," we say, "sit down on a bench, and watch people go by."

When we're honest, we have to admit that in the looks department, most of us fall somewhere around average. After all, average is, well, average. A lot of kids bad-mouth themselves because of the beauty standards of teen magazines they read and TV sitcoms they watch, but ask them how many of their friends look like Jennifer Aniston or Brad Pitt? Not too many. At the mall you see heavy people, tall people, short people, but almost *no one* who looks like they walked off a primetime TV program.

The best thing we as parents can do is model another way of life— finding love, acceptance, and belonging at home. Though you are just one voice among many, if you have been an involved parent, you still have the strongest, most influential voice. Never forget that you swing the pendulum for your kids in all that you do. Don't sell yourselves short. You've been given a great responsibility in how you see the world. Communicate to your kids that you love them for who they are, zits and all.

As you do this, *please* be honest. If your pubescent girl weighs 160 pounds and is big-boned, you can't say she's petite. She'll probably focus on her broad shoulders because they grate against the stick-thin ideal of what our society currently calls beautiful, but her personhood doesn't begin or end with her shoulders. Focus on her great qualities—soft eyes, silky hair, and peaches-and-cream skin tone—while emphasizing her qualities that aren't physical, such as integrity, dependability, compassion, and so on.

I (Dr. Leman) had a lot of zits as a kid, and I *still* get zits once in a while. That's why I tell people to be careful what they pray for. I asked God to keep me looking young, and God gave me zits!

Body Type

Your child's body type has nothing to do with her fitness level, her weight, or her height, but everything to do with her genes. Body type depends on bone structure, which is genetically predetermined, and bone structure can never be changed through diet or exercise.

The fact that your child can't fit into a certain label's clothes does not mean that she has a flaw in her body, but rather that differences exist between her body and that brand's standard sizes. Standards in clothing are based on averages, and averages have nothing to do with beauty.

The awareness that everyone—including celebrities—have different body types can help kids immensely. It means something to a girl to know that though she may never appear on the cover of *Cosmopolitan,* her pear-shaped body type is the same as that of Jennifer Lopez and Cindy Crawford.

Researchers have come up with a variety of ways to categorize the various body types. One method compares body types to different shapes: the triangle, inverted triangle, rectangle, and hourglass. But we like to refer to the body types by foods whose shapes more organically reflect the curves of the human body: the pear, apple, potato, and peanut.

Knowing your body type can help you decide what kinds of clothes to buy, as some colors, fabrics, and patterns look better on certain body types. In general, dark colors help make a part of the body seem smaller, while light colors make that part seem larger. Pears, for example, should consider wearing dark colors below the waist and lighter colors above; vice versa for apples.

The Four Basic Body Types

1. Pear: Hips are wider than shoulders, and most of the weight is carried below the belt. Girls with pear-shaped bodies are heavier in the hips and thighs and smaller in the breasts and shoulders; guys typically have big thighs and are smaller in the chest and shoulders. This body type is also called a triangle.

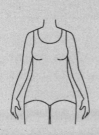

2. Apple: Larger through the bust and midriff than in the hips. People with apple-shaped bodies have small arms and legs and big waists; most of the weight is carried in the chest and abdomen. This body type is also called an inverted triangle.

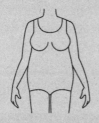

3. Potato: Little or no waist definition. Those with potato-shaped bodies may be rounded or slender; if slender, they tend to have straight figures with no curves. This body type is also called an oval or a rectangle.

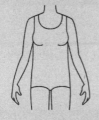

4. Peanut: Waist is smaller than the breast/chest and the hip or thigh areas. People with peanut-shaped bodies have well-defined waists and flat tummies. This body type is also called an hourglass.

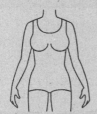

For peanuts, fitted clothing and belts that draw attention to the waist tend to look impressive. For potatoes, belts worn under jackets can provide instant waists for rectangular-shaped bodies, though it can also make heavier, more rounded bodies look even more rounded.

Beauty queen Lakita Garth knows physical beauty is a gift of grace—nothing more. "Nina Blanchard, one of the most respected modeling agents in the world, once told me, 'It's like winning a crap shoot. At the point of conception you won the lottery due to a random selection of genes your parents provided.'"[2] Some people are given striking good looks by God; some aren't.

Our looks, abilities, and relationships often aren't what we want them to be. Disappointment is a part of life; kids must learn how to deal with it as they embrace the new bodies they begin to develop in puberty. This will not be the last time they will feel let down in life! Women's bodies often sag after having a baby; many men develop potbellies and lose their hair. If our children don't figure out what they can do with what they have, when they get older they'll always be chasing elusive "solutions" (plastic surgery, fad diets, liposuction, the latest fad exercises).

What Does the Perfect Body Look Like?
Do Barbie and Ken Have "Perfect" Figures?

To look like a Barbie doll, a 5' 2" woman weighing 125 pounds would need to:

- Grow 2 feet taller: 7' 2" is a nice height for a female in today's world, right?
- Add 5 inches to her chest
- Lose 6 inches from her waist

To look like a Ken doll, a 6' man weighing 185 pounds would need to:

- Grow 20 inches taller: 7' 8" is a nice height for a male in today's world, right?
- Add 8 inches to his neck
- Add 11 inches to his chest[3]

When we hear kids say, "I hate my face," "I hate my zits," "I hate my butt," we ask them, "Besides proper exercise and a healthy diet, what can you do about it, *really?* Either you learn to live with what you have, or you'll feel miserable for the rest of your life. There is nowhere you can go to buy these things you hope to replace."

Many kids will still say, "I'll starve myself before I'll have a butt like that." And those are the ropes that will hang them.

The changes in our kids' bodies go far beyond changing shapes, of course; puberty also affects how our kids smell.

What's That Smell?

A deeply concerned principal called me (Kathy) into the school office one sunny Arizona afternoon.

"We have a little problem here, Mrs. Bell. One female student has a significant body-odor problem. We have tried all the usual hints and have staged conversations about new body products that teens like; we even brought samples to school and passed them out to everyone so that this girl would not be singled out. But the situation is still bad. I am surprised students have not started teasing her. We are at a loss as to what we should do next. What do you suggest?"

Kids in puberty no longer smell like dirt; they stink like wet rats crawling around in the sewer. Parents and teachers may wonder, *How did an entire locker room get into these kids' shoes?* One third-grade teacher admits she has to use plug-in deodorizers in the classroom! Your kids can probably still remember when they hated taking a bath. Now if they forget, their peers may remind them.

Combating Body Odor

- To prevent body odor, bathe daily, use a deodorant, and wear clean clothes.
- Deodorants are available in creams, roll-ons, sprays, sticks, and gels. Use whichever works and makes you comfortable.
- During puberty, deodorant, rather than antiperspirant, should be used, as kids' glands are still developing. Teens do not need a special brand of deodorant.

But just because kids get in the shower doesn't mean they bathe. This is particularly true of boys, who often don't care if they smell—if they even realize that they *do* smell. Parents have to say to their boy, "Hey, would you change your underwear? You've had the same pair on for two weeks." If your kids don't learn from your directions, the bothersome itch of a yeast infection or a jock itch will remind them that they need to keep things clean and dry down there.

> **Fact**
>
> Hundreds of years ago, people often got sick from using the bathroom and failing to wash their hands before eating.

Other kids are more self-conscious. Meg, now in her thirties, can still remember, decades later, the very moment she realized that a curious smell was her own. Sitting a few desks from the music teacher, she smelled her own odor rising through the neck of her Mickey Mouse sweatshirt. *How far can that stench carry?* she worried as she looked at Lance, who sat beside her.

Putting on too much perfume, deodorant, or antiperspirant can cause problems, as well. In fact, antiperspirants shouldn't be used during early puberty, as kids' sweat glands are still developing and need the freedom to do their thing without getting shut down. Regular washing is the best remedy (as well as using a deodorant, which allows you to sweat, as opposed to an antiperspirant, which is designed to stop sweating).

Of course, good hygiene isn't just about smell; it's also about cleanliness and health. Here's an exercise to help get that idea across.

Hand Washing

Objective: To see where germs hang out and to determine what it takes to remove them.

Materials needed: Cinnamon, cooking oil or Vaseline, cotton swab, towel, and access to a sink.

1. Using the end of a clean cotton swab, put cooking oil or Vaseline on your child's hands. Explain that our hands have natural oils, but since he might have clean hands, you are making sure his hands have oil on them.

2. Sprinkle cinnamon on his hands; the cinnamon represents germs. Since cinnamon is not very water soluble, let him know that if the cinnamon gets on his clothing, he should brush it off without water; otherwise, it will stain his clothing. Cinnamon will irritate the skin, so he should avoid getting cinnamon in cuts.
3. Have him gently rub his hands together for about as long as it takes for him to sing "Happy Birthday" so he can see where the germs hang out.
4. Tell him it takes three things to properly wash his hands and get them clean. Ask him to decide what these three things are while he is washing his hands.
5. Send him to the sink to wash his hands.
6. Discuss the three things it takes to get hands clean. Usually a kid will answer soap, water, and a towel. I remind him that is what little kids do: wash with soap, rinse with water, then wipe all that dirt on the towel! Soap, water, and *friction* (rubbing) are the answers! Rubbing the hands together helps loosen and rid your hands of the germs.

Breast Development

"Mom," your daughter may say one afternoon, concerned she has breast cancer, "I feel a lump in my breast."

Such lumps are most likely breast buds, early signs of breast growth. "Right below your nipple?" you might ask.

"Yeah."

"Those are breast buds. They simply mean your breasts are beginning to grow." If she doesn't mention one growing before the other, you might add, "And if you have only one lump, that's nothing to worry about. One breast will begin growing before the other, and breasts take a few years to reach their full size."

Just as differences exist in body types, so breasts come in many different shapes, shades, and sizes; the biggest determining factor here is genetics. How old you are when your breasts begin to develop doesn't determine how big your breasts will become. Sometimes breasts will grow so fast that girls will get stretch marks, which look like red streaks or scratches.

Encourage your daughter to routinely do breast exams in the shower a few days after the end of each menstrual period. Though the risk for cancerous growth is small at this age, it's still possible for girls (and even boys) to get lumps that may have to be removed; plus, it's a great lifelong habit to develop

Boys are often surprised when they suddenly get breast buds, which are tender and feel like a recovering bruise when hit by a soccer ball or jabbed by a friend. *What are those things doing there?!* your son may wonder.

Gynecomastia, as male breast growth is called, occurs as the pubescent body goes through a hormonal adjustment between male and female hormones. Male breast growth usually happens sometime between fifth and seventh grades, so it's a good idea to discuss this with your son when he is in the fifth or sixth grade. "Sixty-five percent of fourteen-year-olds have some degree of gynecomastia.... In two years, 75 percent of boys have a regression of breast tissue. By three years, 90 percent lose breast growth."[4] But because breast cancer can also strike men, if one breast gets significantly larger than the other and doesn't balance out within a month or two, see a doctor.

Measuring for a Bra (Dr. Leman's Guide for Dads)

"Come on," I told my daughter Hannah, "let's go buy you a nice orange bra with white polka dots."

She rolled her eyes and cringed about fourteen times.

"Hannah, wait a minute," I said. "Would you do that for me again? But do it in slow motion? Real slow." She smiled, because she knew I had caught her. And she exaggeratedly rolled her eyes in slow motion.

Body Measurements

Objective: To observe the proportions of the body.

Materials needed: Tape measure (preferably cloth).

Using the tape measure, find which parts of the body are of equal size. For example, the length of the hand from your longest fingertip to your wrist is usually the length of your face. The length from fingertip to fingertip of your outstretched arms often equals your height. Boys love this game.

"Look, if you need a bra, Daddy can buy you your first bra. I've purchased lots of bras."

I'm one of those weird ducks who believes that a good bit of a child's sexual education and training should come from the opposite-sex parent, in large part because I've sat in many a counseling session, horrified at the wrong information passed down from mother to daughter and from father to son. Who knows how to explain what's going through a boy's mind better than a girl's dad? And who better to explain the mystery of what excites—and turns off—a girl than a boy's mom?

But as we've said, you can't ignore all the body issues and then suddenly start talking about sex. That's why, with three of our four daughters (Lauren isn't quite there yet), I've been with them when they bought their first bra.

While as frightening to many fathers as imprisonment in a fabric store, shopping for a bra can be done. Admittedly, in the stores you will be going to, you will be an island of masculinity in a sea of estrogen. Remember, in most stores you can—and should—ask a saleswoman to help your daughter do the actual measuring.

> ### Bra Care
>
> Wash bras in cool water, using the delicate cycle of the washer. Use a mild soap or detergent, which will make the bra last longer.

Remind your daughter not to wear a thick shirt, because she'll need to be measured for two things: bra size and bra cup size. If you need to measure for a bra on your own, here are the guidelines:

1. Take a deep breath. (Repeat step one as necessary.)
2. Ask for a tape measure from the saleswoman for your daughter, or better yet, ask the saleswoman to assist your daughter.
3. If your daughter is measuring herself, instruct her to measure around her chest, just below the breasts. Add four or five inches to the chest measurement to determine the first part of her bra size. (Remember this number: it is the *bra size;* it'll average between 30 and 38.)
4. Have your daughter measure around her chest, right across her nipples. (Remember this number as well: it is the *cup size.*)

   • If the two measurements are the same (30–30, or 32–32) she will probably need a AA or AAA cup size.

- If the breast measurement is one inch bigger (32–33), she will probably need an A cup size.
- If the breast measurement is two inches bigger (32–34), she will probably need a B cup size.
- If the breast measurement is three inches bigger (32–35), she will probably need a C cup size.
- If the breast measurement is four inches bigger (34–38), she will probably need a D cup size.

If you don't want to measure, you can just guess her size, but she will have more trying on to do! Regardless, your daughter will feel like a young woman when you two head out of that store.

I'll admit, shopping for a bra with your daughter feels uncomfortable, but it can break down some walls. When you are there for her first bra purchase, you'll likely be the one she turns to the first time a boy attempts to take that bra off! You can't ignore your daughter's development and suddenly expect her to confide in you later. Trust and openness develop over time, through life events like this. One girl, who felt so embarrassed at the thought of wearing a bra, resisted her mother's insistence that they get one for her. The daughter simply could not articulate her underlying fear—that someone might notice she was wearing one—leaving her mom to conclude that she was denying she needed a bra at all. Only time together can get to the root of such issues. Make a big event of the outing; take her shopping, buy her a cup of coffee and a cookie afterward, and build valuable intimacy with your daughter.

Awkwardness: Outer Extremity Growth

Think of kids' transition into puberty as trading up with a car. It's as if all their life they've been driving around in a compact car; suddenly they're cruising around in an SUV. By mid-puberty, many kids are scraping the curb and bumping into every corner. They honestly don't know how to navigate with their new bodies.

It's easy to understand why: they have to adjust to arms that extend farther than they used to and legs that are longer, heads that are higher, and so on. The space between the lamp and the coffee table that they've walked between their entire lives suddenly becomes too narrow, and you hear a loud *crash*. If drivers' tests were given for these bodies, most of our kids would flunk!

Hormones influence everything: our children's alertness, fatigue, dexterity, fine and gross motor movement, and eye-hand coordination. Keep in mind, when hormones flood the brain, even the ability to remember things gets impaired. Don't immediately assume that your kids are ignoring you. Rather than giving them a list of things to do, you can help them by saying, "When you're done with that, come tell me, and I'll give you the next item." At times their brains get so loaded with hormones that you have to break down skills for them on the spot. It's not that they don't pay attention or that they ignore you; it's just that at times they simply can't remember because of their hormone-loaded bodies.

In many ways, it's almost like having to learn to walk all over again. Everything feels so exhausting that it helps immensely for kids to get adequate sleep and to eat well during this age. Think of it as gassing up that car that now runs on eight cylinders rather than four. That SUV needs twice as much fuel as the compact car did.

Do you remember how awkward you felt during puberty? Do you remember the horror of it? Kids need to know that being awkward is normal. They already feel incredibly self-conscious about it; it's as if they're completely naked. It's not just their klutziness; it's everything. Your daughter walks into a room as gracefully as she can but feels mortified because she's convinced that everybody knows she's wearing a pad and sees she's now wearing a bra. Your boy swears his zit is as big as his head and tries to slip into a room unnoticed, only to loudly knock over a chair on his way to the back of the room, thereby drawing everybody's attention.

The more you fight it—saying things like, "Do you realize that's the third time you've knocked the lamp over?"—the worse it's going to be for your kid. Here's a better alternative: rearrange the furniture! That might sound extreme, but didn't you do that when you had a baby just learning to walk? Instead of fighting what can't be changed, why not just accept it and make adjustments accordingly?

Attitude

Along with body changes comes a massive attitudinal shift. One mother of a fifth grader confessed, "I thought my daughter was going to crash and burn this year." Her daughter had struggled in mid–elementary school and the mother was bracing herself, certain that the onset of puberty would bring out the worst in her child.

A common belief and fear holds that puberty will bring an unmanageable plague of volatile emotions, arguments from the edge of nowhere, and an activities schedule no human parent could ever keep up with. Ask any adult which years they'd least like to go through again, and the puberty years usually top the list.

It's true pubescent kids *are* more active and verbal; they ask more questions, cry at injustice, and argue because they want the world to be fair. But why do we cast these attitudes and reactions in such negative light? Why do we feel these years will be so tough? Your kid is expressing himself in ways he never has, ways that will help him engage with the world as an adult. In fact, the very things about your growing kid that may drive you the nuttiest are often the marks of a vitality born of God. What you're witnessing is all part of your child's journey to becoming a passionate person created by a passionate God.

When I (Kathy) first began working with this age group, I felt as though I began seeing the face of Christ. Pubescent kids are filled with life, dedicated to various causes, yearning for justice, and they throw their entire beings into their activities. The passion of pubescent kids amazes me.

The world would have kids sexualize that passion, encouraging them to direct it toward each other. Movies and television would have them believe that losing their virginity is cool and that others are "doing it" at an earlier age. But this misdirects a legitimate passion that mirrors the very image of God—Christ's passion for a vibrant yet broken world.

Puberty is an emotional time, painted with the full spectrum from joy to pain, and pubescent kids must work through how to live in this ever-widening world. They are discovering what you and I already know: that the world is a place filled with wonder—and pain; that you *can* make a difference, yet good guys don't always win; and that the good in life is more diverse than they'd ever imagined, though bad things also happen to good people. It is as if they have eaten from the tree of the knowledge of good and evil. They realize the horror in the world, see the plight of some unfortunate people, and begin to understand how fragile life really is. They are scouting the boundaries of human emotions and feel deeply the weight of sorrow as well as the rush of joy. This, too, is part of the passion of Christ.

The world would have us settle for sitcom-like answers to the world's misery, but parents, don't be afraid to have your kids cry at its reality.

They will become deeper people as a result. These issues will get stronger as your kids move toward high school. It is evidence that their hearts are being laid wide open. This is a perfect time to teach kids about who Christ is, to direct them to his heart for the world as they begin to understand their own heart and gifts.

In his book *The Wonder of Girls*, Michael Gurian makes the point that kids' activities during the puberty years may provide a clue to their activities later in life:

> A girl's relationships, intimacies, sports activities, art and musical activities, as well as academic learning during the ten-to-twelve period, have a great likelihood of "sticking" or at least "reappearing" later in her life because of their interconnection with the massive brain growth. There is also a greater likelihood that she will not be as good at things she didn't practice during these two years. This is why, generally, we can say that if she enjoys piano at eleven, she'll probably remain somewhat musical during her life. If she reads a lot at twelve, she'll probably enjoy reading throughout life. If she's in stable relationships at ten, she'll probably feel safer in stable relationships throughout life.[5]

Your child has something written in her heart to do; what is it? As kids begin to feel the heartbeat of Christ in them, encourage them to move outside the box. Christ did, challenging the injustice of society, raising the dead, and doing what God called him to do, often in unconventional ways. We may expect to raise kids with seemingly safe and secure nine-to-five jobs, but what if your kid isn't built like that? Encourage your child to take advantage of opportunities you wish you'd had, but be careful that you don't attempt to live vicariously through her. Let kids grow to be themselves, the kids God made them to be.

A wise single mom who had endured a horrible divorce was raising an adopted son who loved building things out of wood. Unfortunately, he also loved tearing wood apart and often took out his aggression on the interior of their house, banging up the walls and ripping things apart. So she went to the local junkyard, picked up whatever wood she could find, bought a box of nails, and handed her boy a hammer. Taking him to a section of the backyard, she said, "This is your work area. Whatever you see in your mind, build it. If you don't like it anymore, go right ahead and tear it down and build something else." What he created surprised her; he crafted beautiful crucifixes. Their church even used them in its stations of the cross.

"I think the Lord is putting the passion of Christ in him," she said, "because he talks about these crosses. I would have never known it if I hadn't thrown him a pile of wood and said, 'Go for it. Build it.'"

Amber Coffman was ten years old in 1993, when, in her words, "I decided that I wanted to do something." At an age when many kids are still seeing who can blow the biggest bubble with their gum, Amber founded Happy Helpers for the Homeless after doing a school book report on one of Mother Teresa's books. "Mother Teresa did homes: I did lunches," Amber explains. Throughout her teen years, Amber and a group of volunteers made and handed out lunches on the weekends for the homeless in Glen Burnie, Maryland, Amber's home town, and nearby Baltimore. Today, Happy Helpers provides lunches for the homeless in forty-nine states and in several countries.

Amber has been busy ever since. Besides volunteering, she speaks to student groups and other organizations around the country about her work with Happy Helpers and how young people can make a difference in their communities. She has appeared on *Oprah* and *Montel* and has won more than one beauty pageant, including Miss Young America in 1999. Crayola even named two crayons, Purple Heart and True Blue, in Amber's honor.

It may sound like a charmed life, but life hasn't been easy. "I've never known my Dad," Amber said. "There have been tough times." Living with her mother, Bobbie, Amber has known "what it's like to need."

Still, with her mother's caring and firm example, Amber has taken her own difficult experience and looked to the needs of others. "Young people want to find where they fit into society," she said, "and they want adults to take them seriously. They should follow through. They can have such a huge impact on our world."[6]

Do you see how what might initially seem like a negative can be turned into a positive? Attitudinally and physically, your children are going through massive changes. They may start to smell. They may knock over a few lamps or chairs. They may need new clothing—every other month! And they may develop a keener sense of justice.

Lean into these changes. The same girl who holds to her convictions at home may become a great advocate for others in the public square.

The same boy who sometimes seems like a rebel may yet grow up to be a prophet.

That bumbling, zit-faced, smelly teen with shoe stink that could slay an elephant just may become the next president, invent a new cure for cancer, lead a revival, or write a best-selling book.

Wait and see.

Chapter 9

Third Base——Female Changes from the Waist Down

Helping Your Daughter Understand Her Reproductive System

You have to breathe, eat, and drink in order to survive. Your digestive system is crucial to ongoing life; without the active, ongoing process, you'd die in a matter of days.

The same is not true of the reproductive system. You can live ninety years without having sex and still remain healthy. Nobody dies by not using their reproductive system, and even those who do use it do so relatively sparingly; no one spends twenty-four hours a day having sex.

We say this because the male and female genitalia, when it comes right down to it, are just body parts. When discussing the reproductive system with your kids, you don't have to move too quickly to conversation about sexual intercourse. In the course of any human life, the use of a person's genitalia will have much more to do with urinating and having a period than with having intercourse. Reminding yourself of this will help to keep the waist-down material in perspective.

Female Anatomy

Many of us adults face a great challenge in accurately discussing female anatomy because we aren't very familiar with our own bodies! We've met a surprising number of grown men and women who don't have a clue about basic reproductive organs. You can't teach what you don't know. With that in mind, let's go through a series of conversations between a mother and a daughter, designed to introduce the girl to the miraculous body that God has given her.

Ovaries and ova (eggs). "Denise told me we come from eggs."

"That's right."

"Really? I thought she was joking."

"Well, they're not like chicken eggs."

Female Reproductive System

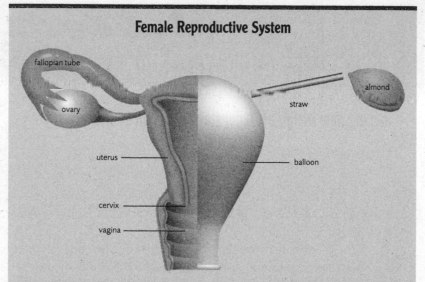

Objective: To understand the size of the ovary and ovum (egg) and to lay out the basic structure of the female reproductive system.

Materials needed: Two almonds in their shells, two packets of sugar, tapioca pudding, two coffee straws cut to 4-inch lengths or one strand of cooked spaghetti cut into two 4-inch strands, one large balloon.

1. *Almonds:* Represent the two ovaries. Half a million eggs are stored inside each ovary, which is roughly the size of an almond in the shell. The eggs, each smaller than a grain of sugar, are released one at a time.

2. *Packets of sugar:* Open one packet for each almond and place the contents next to each almond ovary; each grain of sugar represents a mature egg (ovum).

3. *Tapioca pudding:* Represents what the almond ovaries are like in their consistency inside.

4. Place almonds, coffee straws or strands of cooked spaghetti, and balloon according to the diagram.

5. Using an ink pen, draw a line about three-quarters of an inch up from the neck of the balloon, or open the end of the balloon to show where the cervix would be.

"Oh, I guess I kind of thought that's what she was talking about."

"No, we come from eggs about the size of a grain of that salt you're putting on your omelet."

"That small?! I thought we grew inside."

"We do. That's where the eggs are. They're made and stored in the two ovaries, which are both about the size of an almond in the shell. Here, like this," says the mother, handing her daughter an almond from the cupboard.

"That's not very big."

"Yeah, but do you know how many eggs can fit inside there? There are about half a million potential eggs in each ovary. You are born with all the eggs you need for your whole life. They come out only one at a time, and only about five hundred of them will ever mature over your lifetime. That's why you're so special. Between the two of my ovaries, I guess you could say you're one in million."

"Oh, Mom."

Fallopian tubes. "But where do the eggs go?"

"Well, the ovaries are located at the end of what we call fallopian tubes."

"What are those?"

"Tubes that catch the eggs from the ovaries."

"Why do they have to catch them?"

"Well, the job of these two thin tubes is to catch the eggs from the ovaries and help them travel safely to the uterus."

"Is that where the baby grows?"

"Yes. Each fallopian tube is about four inches long, and about the width of my coffee straw here. Where was that balloon you had the other day? See, the ovaries [almonds] are connected to the uterus [balloon] by the fallopian tubes [four-inch pieces of coffee straws or spaghetti]."

Uterus and endometrium. "But how does a baby fit in there?"

"It doesn't seem like one could, does it? But the uterus, which is hollow and about the size and shape of a pear turned upside down, can stretch to become five hundred times larger to fit the growing baby."

"So the baby really doesn't grow in the stomach."

"No, the uterus is a totally separate body part. Feel the bone below your belly button, almost to your private area?"

"Uh-huh."

"That bone is your pubic bone."

"Do boys have one of those?"

"Yes, but not a uterus. Only women have a uterus, which is there behind the pubic bone. Your dad used to tell me it hurt just to look at me when I was pregnant because my skin had stretched so much. But when you let the air out of the balloon what happens? It goes back to its small balloon shape, doesn't it?"

"Uh-huh."

"So does the uterus. The uterus will expand to fit the baby, but it regains most of its shape, like this balloon, shortly after the baby is delivered. So just because I have a roll on my tummy does not mean my uterus is flapping around inside me. But it sure was big when you were inside! That's one reason why it's important to be married and to be an adult when you have a baby. Your body would not be ready for a job this big just yet. Your job right now is to eat right, grow, and enjoy being a kid. Concentrate on that first!"

"What happens when the eggs aren't fertilized? Do they just fall out?"

"If the egg is not fertilized in the fallopian tube, it dies and disintegrates. The soft lining of blood and tissue on the inside of the uterus, called the endometrium, is shed during a menstrual period if the egg isn't fertilized."

Have your daughter hold a basketball to her abdomen. Ask, "Is your body physically able to carry a baby yet?"

Cervix. "So where does the baby come out?"

"When it's ready, it passes through the cervix, which connects the uterus to the vagina. The cervix is located at the bottom part of the uterus, and it's there to protect the inside of the uterus. Within the cervix are little pockets, called cervical crypts, where mucus is produced."

"Mucus sounds pretty gross."

"It may sound gross. But every opening to the body has something to keep it moist and clean. The eyes have tears, the ears have wax, and the

Bladder

Objective: To see how much urine the bladder holds.

Materials needed: 12-ounce soda cup.

Fill the soda cup; that's approximately how much urine your child's bladder can hold (approximately 1–1.5 ounces of urine per year of your child's age).

Uterus

Objective: To understand the size of a woman's uterus during pregnancy.

Materials: Softball, basketball, beachball (or balls of comparable size).

Use the various balls to show the growth of the uterus throughout pregnancy:

1. *Three months:* softball.
2. *Six months:* basketball.
3. *Nine months:* between basketball and beachball (possibly twins in beachball-size uterus).

---

nose has mucus. The vagina is no different. The mucus helps keep it moist and clean."

Vagina. "And the vagina is where the baby comes out?"

"Yes. The baby passes through the vagina, which is an elastic passageway just below where your urine comes out."

"There's a whole lot more down there than just a single hole, isn't there?"

"You're right about that. The vulva is what we call the entire genital area of the female. It consists of two openings: the urethra, from which you urinate, and the vagina, the opening from which a baby comes out. Pubic hair surrounds this area and grows in an upside-down triangle shape between a woman's legs. The vagina is behind the urethra but not as far back as the rectum, and the urethra and the vagina are surrounded by folds of skin. Girls are different in that they have three openings in the pubic area, while boys have only two."

You may not cover everything in one discussion, and that's okay. You'll have other chances. But staying attentive to opportunities and knowing your material will help make the conversation all the more natural when it does come up.

The Story of Menstruation

For your daughter, blood has always meant one thing—I'm hurt, there's something wrong, pain. But menstruation gives blood a whole new meaning.

Because menstruation is foreign territory to her, thinking about blood differently may be so overwhelming that your daughter may forget anything that has to do with hygiene. *Do you mean blood is going to come out of there?!* she may wonder. *How much blood? Does it gush out? Do you pee it out? Can you stop it? Does it hurt?*

"Mom," she might ask, "how do I know when that's all going to start?"

"You'll notice changes in your body," you might reply. "Your breasts will start to grow, hair will start to grow under your arms and in the pubic area, and your body shape will change. You will begin to notice mucus on your underwear or when you wipe. These are all clues from your body that it's preparing for your first menstrual period."

"When will that happen?"

"Well, first the pituitary gland must send the chemical messengers, estrogen and progesterone, to tell the rest of your body to 'wake up' and grow. Those little chemical messengers will be in your bloodstream for up to three years or so before any physical changes."

"You mean that stuff is in my bloodstream three years before my period?"

"Yeah, it takes time for your body to mature."

Both you and your daughter will begin to notice changes in her eating habits and moods. One girl realized that she started slamming her bedroom door before each period.

Three things must happen for a girl's period to start. A message needs to get to the ovaries to tell an egg to mature, to the uterus to tell its inner lining to thicken, and to the cervix to tell it to change the consistency of the mucus.

> **Fact**
>
> The female egg is about the size of the period at the end of this sentence.

Every month a mature female's body will make a special lining, the endometrium, in the uterus. Usually only one egg from one ovary will actually mature, and nature determines which ovary will be selected to mature the egg. However, during the first six to twelve months of your daughter's period, she will not always produce and release an egg; in other words, she will not always ovulate. In fact, roughly half the time she won't, so that her ovary is building up pressure for nothing. That pressure creates a physiological feeling inside your daughter when the pressure is building, and when that egg does break loose from the ovary, it can hurt.

Because the ovulation process is erratic when a girl begins having her period, she will not have a regular period. In fact, she may have a period and then not have another one for six months or more. This is not the time to trot down to the physician to put her on birth control pills (to regulate her cycle). Her body needs a little space to figure out its own cycle, which can remain erratic for even the first few years. Don't worry; this is normal!

"The pituitary gland also sends messages through the bloodstream to the cervix, where the cervical crypts produce mucus. You know that yellow stuff on your underwear?"

"Yeah."

"Well, that's going to become clear, and as you start seeing it get clearer, it's a sign to you that your period is coming. It will change from pasty white to yellow to clear—kind of like egg white. As you see more of

---

Be Prepared

1. Ovulation can hurt.
2. In puberty, a young girl may not always ovulate (release an egg), which means her period may not be regular at first. This can go on for several years. Keep in mind, your daughter's body is building up pressure in preparation to release an egg; when it doesn't do so, she can be left with a very uncomfortable physiological feeling inside her.
3. Don't trot down to the physician and put your daughter on birth control to regulate her period. Her body simply needs a little space to figure out its own cycle. Encourage healthy living and don't worry if her cycle is "off."

that on your underwear, it's a sign that your period is coming soon. Your body is getting into a pattern that's special for you."

The pituitary gland sends another message to your daughter's uterus. The chemical messengers go to the uterus lining, the endometrium.

"The chemical messengers tell the body to build up a 'bloody bed,' the endometrium, to practice getting ready to have babies. It's like the body is saying, 'I've just started having my period, I'm not married, and I'm not ready for a baby. But I have to practice so that when you do get married, I will be ready to have a baby when it's time. The way I practice is to build up a bloody bed in your uterus and then let it drip out during your period.'"

"But why does it have to get rid of the old bed?"

"It's like changing the sheets. It can't have an old bed for a new baby. And it takes your body time to practice this. That's what happens when you have a period over and over again. The endometrium lining thickens and grows. If a woman gets pregnant, then that lining is needed, so the body keeps it. If she does not get pregnant, the lining comes out of the body as a menstrual period. Having a period is like making the bed again. Just because you start to have periods doesn't mean it's time to have a baby. Your body is simply practicing."

"How much blood comes out? What does it look like? Does it drip out? Does it gush out? Does it pour out of me?"

"It will not come out all at once, just small amounts at a time— about a quarter of a cup to half a cup of menstrual blood per period each cycle. It is normal to notice blood that is a light pink, red, or brownish color on your underpants or on the tissue when you wipe yourself. When you're urinating, you can stop the urine from coming out. But menstrual flow is different from urine. You cannot stop the flow from coming out. That is why feminine pads are needed."

Important Things to Know about Your Daughter's Period

Because of hormonal influences and changing equilibrium in your daughter's body:

- She will probably sleep more.
- She may get nauseated or want to vomit.
- She may even pass out.

"How long will my period last?"

"Every girl's body is a little different. Most girls have a period that lasts from three to five days, but some girls have periods that last seven days. Every girl has her own special cycle, which is measured from the beginning of day one of your period to the beginning of a new period. If you keep a record of your first twelve periods, that will help you figure out which days you can expect your periods."

Pads and Tampons

There are few things more mortifying for a pubescent girl than starting her period at school and having to go to the nurse's office to ask how to put on a pad. When I (Kathy) speak about this at mother-daughter classes, the girls literally cringe at the very thought of such an occurrence. We hope none of our daughters will ever find themselves in this situation. We are thankful that the nurse's office is there if they need it, but it is our job to prepare them for such an event.

We also need to talk to our daughters about other practical matters. For instance, when a girl is having her period and she stands up and feels blood gush from inside, she may swear it's running down her leg even if she's wearing a pad. That's a normal feeling and nothing to worry about; the pad will work.

Many girls feel overwhelmed with the new sensations that menstruation brings—not to mention all that blood! Girls need a lot of support during this time. My daughter Amy used to pass out because of her hormonal imbalance. Other girls may feel the need to vomit because they feel so nauseated. Sometimes the blood flows so strong that girls must change pads after every class, along with every other girl having a period, and there's only five minutes between classes. They may be terrified of being tardy, because what if the teacher asks why? They'd be too embarrassed to explain that they needed to change their pad but the bathroom was too full!

All of these pressures combined mean that by the end of the day, your daughter may be falling apart. If you greet her with "What's wrong now?!" when she needs your understanding most, she'll shut down. Give her extra space and empathy and plenty of time to rest and recover. Pamper her a little; let her watch a favorite movie or TV show or treat her to a cup of tea and honey.

Testing Pads

Objective: To understand how pads hold menstrual blood.
Materials needed: Variety of pads, 1/4–1/2 cup of water, blue food coloring.

1. At a dollar store or local drugstore, buy a variety pack of pads or a few different kinds (wings, maxi, mini, panty liners, etc.).
2. Cut the pads in half to see what they are made of and how they hold blood. (Save at least one of each kind of pad for your daughter to try on.)
3. Fill a measuring cup with about 1/4–1/2 cup of water; color it blue with the food coloring. Dribble this onto the pads to see how well each will absorb the menstrual fluid released during the three to five days of the period. Which seems to work the best?
4. Practice wrapping up the pads so that no one can see them and throw them away.

Not many parents overdo it on encouragement, but you do have to be careful. One girl's mother felt so happy her daughter had begun her period—that she had "become a woman"—that the mother threw a party. When Mary came home and walked into the room, she found that her mom had called together all the neighborhood kids!

"This is for you, Mary! You've become a little woman today!" Kids who didn't have a clue what that meant had gathered around the table to celebrate her emerging womanhood, and the daughter was mortified!

Remember, moms, your daughter cannot wear the pads you wear. You may have figured that when she starts her period, she can just use the pads in your cupboard. But your pads most likely cannot be her pads. She's too little!

Practice. Make sure your daughter has her own pads *before* she starts her period so that when she does, the world doesn't cave in. Go to a dollar store and get as many different pads and tampons as you can. Have her try them on at home and do the things she normally does. It's good for her to have one pad in her locker and one pad in her school backpack so that she's prepared. Mom (and Dad), make sure *you* carry pads or tampons for her in your car glove compartment. You never know when your daughter is going to need help.

Get specific. "Really, Kathy, do you have to get so detailed and specific?" moms ask me.

"Do you remember trying to figure out your first tampon?" I respond.

As basic as pads and tampons are, sometimes the details slip by our kids. Mothers assume girls know they're supposed to wrap up pads and tampons before throwing them away. After all, no one likes to walk into a bathroom and find a used pad lying beside the toilet. And everyone knows that dogs and curious little brothers like to get into pads left lying around, right?

Nope.

You need to be very detailed in your training. Mom and Dad, break it down simply. How do you wrap a pad up? How do you throw it away? It's amazing the amount of detail girls need. One girl asked, "How does the blood know to go down to the pad?" Those little girls may think that

Trying on Pads

Objective: To see which pad best fits your daughter's body and activities *before* she starts her period.

Materials needed: Variety of pads.

1. In the privacy of your home, have your daughter try on a variety of pads. If the pad has a removable piece of paper, there is usually a sticky adhesive underneath the paper. The sticky side goes on the underwear. Place the pad so that the main part covers the crotch area of the underwear.
2. Have her wear various pads around the house. If she rides a bike or rides horses, have her try wearing the pads during these activities to see whether they feel comfortable.
3. Get a small bag and put a few of the pads of choice in it. Have her keep these in her locker or school backpack, as well as some at home. You should also keep a few pads in your car glove compartment for emergencies.
4. Have your daughter think through how she is going to get the pad from her locker to the bathroom.

Using Tampons

Objective: To understand how to wear and dispose of a tampon correctly.

Materials needed: Tampons, if your daughter must wear them. Tampons are needed during swimming and certain other sports activities. Make sure your daughter lets you know if she is using a tampon.

1. Have your daughter use a hand mirror to see where a tampon would go.
2. Tampons are placed inside the vagina, all the way up to the cervix. You insert the tampon into the vagina with your fingers or by pushing on the applicator. A tampon has a string that hangs out of the vagina so that you can remove it. If your daughter puts it in only part way, it's going to hurt. It's got to go all the way up. Helpful directions come inside every box.
3. Tampons need to be changed every four hours and should not be worn at night or when there is only a light flow.

if the string breaks on their tampon, they'll lose it up inside their body— perhaps into their stomach or up into their throat. Who knows? (They sure don't.) They need to know that if an entire baby can come out of there, they can put their fingers up, find it, and pull it out.

One day when I was working at the hospital, I thought I would get pads from the nurses to show the girls the various sizes of pads women wear after they have a baby. And those pads look like Depends.

"Why do you have those, Kathy?" the nurses asked.

I began telling them, and immediately they said, "Thank goodness you're teaching people about this! We had a lady up here today, and we had to explain menstruation to her. She just had a baby, but she didn't even know how she had a period, so we were trying to explain a few things about what was happening to her body. You wouldn't believe how many times we get women on this floor who are having babies but haven't a clue how their bodies work."

Be cautious with tampons. "There's no way you're wearing a tampon," one physician mother told her daughter. But when the daughter got with one of her girlfriends who had a couple of tampons, they thought they would be cool. Defying her mother's authority, she and her friend took the strings and tied the tampons onto their underwear. They didn't have a clue how it was supposed to catch blood, but they felt so proud to be wearing them!

That mother had a reason for her caution. Women and girls who use tampons and don't change them regularly can be at risk of getting toxic shock. That's why tampons should be used by pubescent girls only when swimming or during other such activities. To help avoid the risk of toxic shock syndrome, change tampons every four hours and do not wear them to bed; instead, allow the blood to flow freely from the body with a pad. And remind your daughter to always let an adult know she is wearing a tampon, in case she does begin exhibiting symptoms of toxic shock.

Toxic Shock Syndrome

I (Kathy) knew of one little girl, the daughter of one of the local teachers in our small hometown, who began exhibiting the flu-like symptoms of toxic shock syndrome. When her blood pressure dropped, those around her knew her condition was deteriorating and called an ambulance to take her to the hospital.

In the ambulance, the young girl looked at her mother. "Is this really serious?" she asked.

"I don't know," her mom said.

"Mommy, am I going to die?" she asked.

"Sweetheart," her mom said, "I don't think so—I hope not."

She fell deeper into toxic shock during the ambulance ride and died before they reached the hospital. The news hit our community hard.

Help for Dads

Tampons are different than sanitary pads. *Pads,* made from absorbent layers of cotton with a built-in plastic lining, are flat and are usually affixed to the underpants by a sticky strip that keeps them firmly in place. Pads come in different sizes, thicknesses, and even shapes. *Tampons* are made of soft cotton or other fibers pressed together into a firm, compact cylinder that is inserted into the vagina to soak up menstrual fluid.

Toxic shock syndrome (TSS), though rare, is extremely serious, and as in this little girl's case, it can be deadly. Bacteria grows where stagnant blood is kept in a moist and dark environment. You can get TSS from packing a nose bleed too long when hiking, from a cut on the arm bandaged too long, or from countless other scenarios in which blood is allowed to connect with the right bacteria or germs to produce TSS.

When high-absorbency tampons came out, we thought it was great! We didn't have to change our tampons until we were home from school. The problem was that the vagina provides the perfect breeding ground for bacteria when given time to stick around. Since high-absorbency tampons need changing less frequently, they create the conditions that can lead to toxic shock.

Toxic Shock Syndrome (TSS) Can Be Deadly

Symptoms:

- Fever over 102 degrees
- Faintness or dizziness
- Diarrhea
- Nausea or vomiting
- Sunburn-like rash that is painless

If you are using a tampon and have any of these symptoms, remove the tampon and get immediate medical attention. TSS can be life-threatening.

- There seems to be a link between tampon use and the prevalence of TSS; TSS may be linked to the acid-base balance in a woman's body.
- TSS seems to be linked to how long a tampon is worn. Change a tampon every four hours. Don't use tampons during the night while you are sleeping. If you use tampons, use small ones and change them frequently. Read the tampon box and purchase tampons made from nonchlorine-bleached cotton or rayon. Do not purchase superabsorbent tampons. To avoid pinching from a plastic applicator, make sure the tampon is completely inside of the applicator.
- As much as possible, use a pad instead of a tampon.

Make sure your girls tell you they're wearing a tampon. Even some regular-absorbency tampons have super-absorbency material, which means kids should stay on top of changing their tampons. As new users, they must change their tampon every four hours. Medically, the Academy of Obstetrics and Gynecology and the Academy of Pediatrics say at least every six hours, but we're being more conservative with this age group. Instruct your daughter to put the tampon in during the morning and to change it for a new one during her lunch break. After school, she should change it again.

Before you allow your daughter to use a tampon, ask yourself a few questions: Does your daughter consistently do what she says she's going to do? What's her track record? Does she put away that makeup bottle? If she doesn't follow through on simple tasks, I'd be very careful about giving her a hygienic option in which indifference or forgetfulness is literally a matter of life and death.

New users should use tampons only when absolutely necessary: when swimming, horseback riding, or in gymnastics class. Never wear tampons at night, and never wear them during light days. The body needs the free flow of blood; that's how it cleanses itself.

Journeying into No-*Man's*-Land: A Dad's Guide to Buying Pads

For a man, buying pads or tampons ranks up there with asking his buddies if they'd like to switch over to the home-gardening channel during Super Bowl commercials. Face it, ladies, guys simply don't want to venture into the feminine-hygiene aisle. The very word *feminine,* prominently displayed at the end of the aisle, makes it the equivalent of a military no-fly zone for men.

"I walked down the feminine-hygiene aisle," said one dad who went with his daughter to buy pads, "thinking, *Where do we even begin?*"

Just what *do* you do, dads, when your wife is away at the church women's retreat for the weekend and your sixth-grade daughter says, "Daddy, I just had my first period today"? What are you going to buy? Moms, would your husband have the composure—and the know-how—to handle the situation?

Dads, if you have a daughter approaching puberty—or already in the puberty years—who hasn't yet started her period, you'd better start wandering that aisle. Make that turn on your way to pick up chips and salsa for Sunday's game.

I (Dr. Leman) learned my lesson early on in marriage. One night Sande sang out with that "Honey Do" tone, "Honey, would you go down to Walgreens for me?"

"For what?" I replied—a reasonable question, I thought, given that It was ten o'clock at night.

"Well, I just started my—"

"Oh, no!" I said, "I'm not going to buy *those,* woman. I love you, but I *ain't* doing that."

Well, ten minutes later I'm standing in the feminine-hygiene aisle at Walgreens, getting all kinds of mischievous stares from the woman behind the cash register. If you haven't been to this aisle, guys, there are more pads and tampons than there are Bowl games. I bought a box that I thought looked familiar and brought it back, the victorious hunter returning home from the hunt.

"Honey, those are the wrong kind," Sande told me. "They won't work."

Now it was 11:00, and Walgreens was closed. I headed off to the twenty-four-hour store, and by the time I got there, I didn't want to have to set foot in another feminine-hygiene aisle. I bought a box of everything they had: Regular. Curved. Pantiliners. Long Super Maxis. Super absorbency. Super plus absorbency. Ultra-thin with wings. Ultra-thin without wings. Light days. Rainy days. Heavy days.

You wouldn't believe the looks I got holding nearly eighty dollars of feminine hygiene products in my arms at 11:15 on a Sunday night, appearing like I was buying out the feminine-hygiene products.

"Here, find what you need," I said when I got home. "I'm not going back to that store again."

I have to admit, however, that this was good practice for when my daughters started their periods. If you never become familiar with this aisle, you may have to scramble, as one dad we know who needed to shop for his daughter and had to phone his wife to learn what to buy; he was in Arizona and his wife was traveling in California!

Take it in stride. Dad, imagine how you would feel if, as a child, your mom were walking you through how to wash your sheets after your first wet dream. Can you imagine a more humiliating or embarrassing event? Your daughter will probably feel the same if she is forced to approach you about her period. She needs you to take it in stride, to assure her that what she's going through isn't anything to be ashamed of.

In other words, your sense of empathy, concern, and relationship are just as important as your knowledge. If you use humor effectively, use it here. Let her know that you're not uncomfortable and she's not an outcast.

"I know what this is," Frank told his daughter, with whom he had already had several conversations about the changes she was going through. "You're going to be okay. These things happening to you are a natural part of life. You're growing up. It's okay." Frank's daughter cuddled up to him, and he held her like she was still his little girl.

Emergency assistance! Let's assume for a moment, Dad, that this is the only section of this book that you're reading because your daughter just came to you for help. It's evening and you need to get to the store to buy something before it closes.

When this happened to my (Kathy's) brother, he began reading boxes as he stood there in that testosterone-forsaken aisle, and his daughter wandered up and down the aisle thinking, *I don't know what to choose, Dad. I don't know what to choose.*

What *should* one look for when buying feminine-hygiene products?

1. For a first period, buy pads rather than tampons. The experience of putting a pad in the panties is less traumatic than figuring out how to put a tampon inside the vagina. Slow down and read the packaging. There is no time limit for shopping in grocery stores.
2. Look for teen products. The good news is that companies have finally caught on to a young woman's particular needs. A whole array of teen sizes exists for all sorts of hygiene products. While many of these products use the teen label simply as a gimmick,

---

Pad Shopping for Dads

- Go down that grocery store aisle you never set foot in—the feminine-hygiene aisle.
- Look for packages that say *slender, slim, mini, thin,* or anything else that suggests a small size.
- Slow down. Grocery stores don't have a time limit.
- When in doubt, buy a few kinds and take them home for your daughter to try out.

---

pads and tampons are one product that benefit from the focus. Your teen may not be able to wear your wife's pads, but packages labeled *slender, slim, mini,* and *thin* are all good bets, as is anything else that suggests a small size.

3. Lastly, if you're a dad in the store buying pads for your daughter's first period—unless you've already prepared and know which pads fit her best—you'll probably want to buy a few kinds so that when you get home, she'll have what she needs, in spite of your inexperience.

You'll still be the hero come to save the day.

What Every Kid Needs

At times, such as when Dad braves the feminine-hygiene aisle to buy his daughter's pads, it seems girls and boys couldn't be more different. "Sugar and spice and everything nice," the saying goes, "that's what girls are made of." Boys, on the other hand, are all "snakes and snails and puppy dog tails." One is primping in front of the bathroom mirror with her friends while the other is rearranging the living-room furniture as he wrestles his buddies. Yet while physically and emotionally boys and girls are different, they are similar in the nourishment they need: love, acceptance, belonging, and open communication. As different as boys and girls may appear, many of the issues they face are the same.

If you do not have a son, we recommend that you read the next chapter anyway so that you'll be better able to talk with your daughter about male anatomy. Regardless, we strongly suggest that before moving on you first read the section on talking with your pubescent child about masturbation, located toward the end of chapter 10. The thought of even bringing up the topic—especially to your daughter—may surprise some of you, but as we've said all along, talking openly and honestly about these issues not only helps your child anticipate what lies ahead; it will help her make good decisions when those issues are before her.

Third Base—Male Changes from the Waist Down

Helping Your Son Understand His Reproductive System

Dr. Leman has a favorite thing to do when asked to talk at a school on reproductive health. He loves to shock everybody by bringing out a blackboard and asking the audience to call out slang names for the penis. Boys are notorious for inventing all sorts of names for various parts of the body, but you could write an encyclopedia on slang names for the penis alone. It's not difficult to fill up an entire board within just a minute or two.

Next he says, "Now tell me some slang names for the female genitalia."

Without fail, there's an awkward pause—as there should be. We're not quite as comfortable encroaching on a woman's modesty to mention those words in public. Dr. Leman then talks to the kids about why it's important to maintain this reticence.

While boys eagerly talk jokingly about Mr. Johnson, the one-eyed snake, or little willy, talking seriously about sensitive body parts is another matter entirely. That's why it's crucial for you parents to be comfortable yourself in order to put your boy at ease when talking about sexual reproduction. The best way to do this, as we've already said many times, is to take life in stride and to use kitchen-table sex ed to make sexual discussions seem normal and routine.

What follows is some helpful information to help guide you through conversations about the male reproductive system. If you do not have a daughter and skipped the previous chapter, we recommend that, at some point, you go back and read it so that you'll be better able to talk with your son about the female reproductive system.

The Male Reproductive System

Penis and erections. Pubescent boys can get an erection about as easily as Barry Bonds can swing a bat. The strangest things can cause a "full salute": a spring breeze, the walk down the courtyard steps toward the lunchroom, the homeroom teacher entering the classroom (for whom they have absolutely *no* attraction), the sight of a girl's bra straps through her shirt, a girl sitting in their lap.

This "ever ready" state results because the developing male body is simply trying to figure out its own growth, first sending too many hormones, then sending too few hormones. Between boyhood and manhood, many of these chemical messengers are being sent to the genitals. This can cause great embarrassment; we've talked to many boys who sat in class with an erection that felt as large as the state of California and, at exactly that moment, were called upon to give a report in front of the class, or some other embarrassing episode occurred.

"Don't worry," you might say. "Most people won't notice, and erections subside pretty quickly. Just don't wear jeans or pants that are too tight, and if it's becoming a regular problem, think about wearing a shirt that hangs low. If you do that, no one will notice."

Just as a young woman needs to alter her dress to cover her growing cleavage, so a boy in the thick of puberty needs to conceal the inevitable erections.

"Yeah, but why do erections happen like that?" your son may ask.

"Well, the penis is made of soft, spongy tissue—kind of like a kitchen sponge—and blood vessels. At first when your body is changing, those little chemical messengers—the ones that influence your hair with bad-hair days and your skin with an occasional pimple—will also travel to your penis, telling it to 'grow up.' Every part of your body has to change from a boy's body to a man's body. Your body sends signals that fill your penis with blood; that's what makes it hard and erect."

"Yeah, I know! I was just sitting there in class today when the teacher called on me to give my report and it happened!"

"Sometimes as a boy's body is developing, hormonal signals get crossed. Spontaneous erections happen every night when you sleep, and sometimes they happen during the day as well. You can't do anything about that. Your body has hormones flooding through it, and sometimes erections just happen at random."

Testes and scrotum. Every male knows that the place of greatest pleasure can also be the place of greatest pain. In a woman's body, the reproductive organs are tucked safely inside, protected by the pubic bone.

In a young boy, they're hanging out there for any ball to hit, and for a guy, *nothing* hurts as much as taking a hit below the belt.

That's why wise Little League coaches require players to wear athletic cups. One coach we know laughed a bit at this restriction. He

> ## Fact
>
> Each testis contains four hundred to six hundred tubules, and the length of each tubule is over two feet long. If the tubules were stretched out end to end, they would be about as long as three football fields!

had played football at the university level and admitted, "I really don't see the need for it with such a young group of boys, but since those are the rules, we'll follow them."

It's a good thing he did. During one of the first games, a boy got hit in the groin with a fastball. Everyone in the stands and on the field heard the shocking sound as the baseball hit and bounced off the boy's cup.

"Well, it's a good thing I had that!" the boy said as he thumped his cup with his bat, and everybody laughed.

All males can relate with a wince to an athlete they see speared, punched, or thrown a curveball in the groin. Every boy has his story about getting hit in the crotch. But what most boys don't know, and should know, is that if one of his testicles begins to grow larger than the other following such an injury, he should tell an adult.

"Remember that time you jumped the ditch on your bicycle and got hit in the groin by the handlebars?"

"Yeah."

"That's where your sperm is produced, so it's a sensitive area. You already know it hurts. But if one testicle ever suddenly gets much larger than the other one after an injury like that, make sure you tell someone. Tell me or Mom, the school nurse, or someone else in charge. Don't just tell your friend."

Explain that one testicle usually hangs a little lower than the other and is generally a bit larger than the other. Unless there is a *major* difference, there is no cause for concern. During childhood the testicles are about the size of a large, oval marble, but during puberty each testicle grows to about the size of a walnut.

Inside the testicles, a lot of sperm-making is going on. Each testis contains four hundred to six hundred tubules; each tubule is over two feet long and is about the thickness of a piece of thread. If the tubules were stretched end to end, they would be about as long as three football fields!

The average male produces about three hundred million sperm *per day* in these tubules, and those sperm will continue to mature as they travel through the rest of the reproductive system, from the testes through the epididymis, then through the vas deferens, and out through the penis's urethra. Unused sperm will get reabsorbed in the testicle, stored in the seminal vesicle, or released during a nocturnal emission (what boys commonly call a wet dream). Boys (and adults) may be surprised to know that once the pituitary gland tells a boy's body to create sperm during puberty, it will not stop until the day he dies.

Because the testicles lie outside the body, they are vulnerable to climatic changes. Most boys notice early on that their scrotums shrivel up when they jump into cold water. This is all part of the scrotum's job to protect the sperm-making process.

"You know what the scrotum is, right?"

"Yeah, the pouch that holds the testicles."

"Right. Well, sperm is produced there, and it has to be kept at just the right temperature. The scrotum responds to heat or cold. To keep the testicles warm, it moves tighter against the body. To keep the testicles cool, it relaxes further away from the body."

Overly tight underwear or pants can impede this process, so boys should be warned accordingly.

Epididymis and vas deferens. "The epi-what?"

Most boys probably aren't going to be familiar with the epididymis and the vas deferens unless they've recently gone through reproductive science class.

Once sperm are made in the testes, they mature in the *epididymis*. The epididymis is a tightly coiled tube that connects each testicle to the vas deferens. If stretched out, the epididymis would be about twenty feet long. It takes between eighteen hours and ten days for the sperm to mature in the epididymis, and this is where they are stored for up to a month before moving on.

The *vas deferens* are long, narrow eighteen-inch tubes that are about as flexible as strands of cooked spaghetti. These tubes start at the epididymis and wind over the bladder to the urethra. The sperm are propelled from the epididymis through this pipeline. The wide part of the vas deferens stores sperm for a few hours to several months. Sperm cells that are not ejaculated get reabsorbed.

Male Anatomy

Objective: To understand the makeup of the male reproductive system.

Materials needed: A spongy hair curler or kitchen sponge, two big marbles, a baby sock, and a 100-yard spool of thread.

- Use the spongy hair curler or kitchen sponge to give your boy an idea of what the penis tissue is like inside. When this tissue fills with blood, it becomes hard.
- *Marbles and baby sock:* Place two marbles inside the baby sock to represent the scrotum and testes. You will notice that one marble (testis) will usually hang lower than the other, this is normal.
- *Spool of thread:* Unravel the whole spool of thread. The thread represents the tubules in the testes where the sperm is produced. Imagine that approximately *two* spools of thread are in *one* testicle. That is a lot of sperm-making machinery!

The prostate gland is a muscular, glandular organ that surrounds the urethra at the base of the bladder. It secretes the liquid part of the semen, which aids in the sperm's life and movement.

Seminal vesicle, semen, and the urethra. The *seminal vesicle* is a tiny gland located behind the widest part of the vas deferens. It produces seminal fluid that helps the sperm get where they are going and also protects them and nourishes them with nutrients.

Semen is a mixture of seminal vesicle fluid, glandular secretions, and sperm. The *urethra* is the passageway out of the male body for sperm and urine, and semen moves from the prostate gland to the urethra.

"But how can urine and semen go out the same place?"

"There's a valve around the bladder that shuts off during an erection. That way urine does not mix with sperm in the urethra."

Jockstraps and Athletic Cups

We know of one little boy—not quite yet a pubescent—whose coach told him he couldn't practice anymore until he wore a cup. The boy went into the bathroom, pulled out a Dixie cup, then went to his mom and said, "This is really embarrassing; besides, I don't see how it's going to do anything."

The mom laughed in spite of herself and took him to the store to pick out a real one. Her son put it in his backpack, then later called her at work during lunch.

"Mom, I've been worrying all day; does the cup go inside my underwear, or outside?"

She didn't have a clue, and her husband wasn't available, so she made a frantic call to her father, who gave her the proper instructions.

Just as men need to be ready to talk bras and tampons, so caring moms need to be prepared to talk cups. It's okay to ask for help, moms. I (Kathy) felt mortified when I went to buy my son, John, a cup, but I took it in stride, mainly because I didn't want him to feel embarrassed. When we walked into the store and looked around I thought, *I have absolutely no idea what I'm doing.* Of course, my son didn't know what he was doing either, but he acted as if he did.

We approached it from a why-don't-you-educate-us point of view and joked together about the whole experience. "How do we do this?" we asked the salesperson. I broke the ice by asking questions I figured both of us had: "Is there anything you have to get used to? Is it comfortable? What is this thing made of?" I figured that if John saw me asking questions, he might feel comfortable enough to begin asking his own embarrassing questions; we had plenty of time for both of us to die of embarrassment when we got in the car, out of sight of the salesperson.

All in all, ladies, you have it pretty easy. A cup might look a little strange to you, but purchasing one is easier than buying a first bra. Simply find a clerk and say, "We need one of those athletic cups. He's playing

Help for Moms

Jockstraps and athletic cups are not the same thing. *Jockstraps,* also called athletic supporters, are used to support the male genitalia and keep them firmly against the body. Wearing a "jock" is required for many sports. *Athletic cups* are hard cups that fit inside the jockstrap to cover the male genitalia and help prevent injuries. In baseball and many other sports, wearing a cup is required.

Little League." They do come in different sizes, and your son may insist on an extra large, but a small will suffice this time around. Regardless, when you walk out of that store, he's going to feel like a little man with armor plating.

Wet Dreams

In the desert outside Tucson, dry streambeds, or what we call washes, fill with water during the summer rains. It's not uncommon among the mountain foothills for highways to intersect with these washes, dipping into their channels where the highway crosses them.

We know of one father and his son of five or six who were driving along the highway when they came to one wash with particularly steep banks. As the car dropped into the dip and then went up the other side, the boy considered the roller coaster–like experience and said, "Hmmm ... That makes my penis feel good."

The fact that your kindergarten-age boy is having sensual feelings in his little penis is a telltale clue of what God knew all along: we are sexual beings from day one. For many moms, that's a shock. But that curveball is also a perfect opportunity in conversation to naturally introduce the topic of sexual intimacy in marriage.

Parents, when your son reaches that inevitable night when he wakes up from one of the most arousing dreams of his life—something he had no control over, mind you—with semen in his pants from a nocturnal emission, do you want your kid to be guilt-ridden, confused, and embarrassed? Or do you want your kid to think, *This must be what Mom talked about?* By informing him ahead of time that it will happen, you take away guilt and affirm that Dad and Mom just might know what they're talking about after all. It might even start your son wondering, *What else have they got to tell me?*

For a boy to ejaculate during a dream, he obviously has to be dreaming about something physically pleasurable. Ask any man to tell you about his first wet dream, and he could probably tell you about it scene by scene—with a smile on his face. I (Dr. Leman) was around thirteen when I had my first wet dream, and I still remember it to this day. By telling your kid about this experience, you're preparing him for something that could otherwise be traumatic.

Sex is not bad. Please don't communicate that it is! It's even better than good; it's *great!* We need to tell kids that just as God has a wonderful way of getting females ready for reproduction with their periods, he has a way of preparing the male body for reproduction: a nocturnal emission. As males become capable of reproduction, the body makes sperm and stores it in a reservoir until it is released in a whitish, sticky liquid called semen to make way for more sperm. In the same way that the lining of a woman's uterus gets released in her menstrual flow to make way for another egg, a young man's sperm gets released so that his body can produce more. As a way of releasing this overflow of sperm, almost all pubescent boys will have what we call wet dreams, or nocturnal emissions.

There's one other way (besides sex) for sperm to be released. Sooner or later, you're going to have to come to grips with the m-word.

Masturbation

Most of what we've talked about has not been controversial. But now we'll dive into a subject full of controversy: masturbation.

How much should you tell your pubescent son or daughter (yes, this applies to girls as well as boys) about masturbation? *A little*. That might sound like a cop-out, but we've found that many parents make the mistake of not talking about it at all, while other parents focus on it too much. Determine your values, talk about them with your spouse to assure you're in agreement, then talk with your kid, but don't put too much focus on it.

When one of the Leman daughters was about three, she had this way of putting her thumbs together, inverting her hands, and doing the bump-and-grind on the floor while watching *Sesame Street*. I'm sure Oscar the Grouch never had such an audience!

The scene horrified my wife, Sande. "Honey, you're the psychologist—do something!" she said.

We hadn't covered this scenario in our graduate school practicum. What do you do in such situations with a three-year-old—call 911? "Somebody come over quick! My daughter is doing the bump-and-grind in front of *Sesame Street*!"

I don't think so.

I walked over and nonchalantly led her to her room. "If you're going to touch yourself like that," I explained, "you need to touch yourself in your own room, not while you're with everyone else." That's all I said to her—and very matter-of-factly, without launching into a drawn-out lecture about the labia and the clitoris or about sexual mores.

Parents often imagine their kids to be nonsexual until their wedding night. Then, suddenly, *wham, bang,* the couple is somehow magically transformed into sexual beings as soon as they speak their wedding vows. In truth, we're sexual from day one. What are you going to communicate to your kids about this, knowing that they are sexual creatures *today?*

Many past prohibitions about masturbation were based on nonsense. You don't go blind masturbating, or develop hair between your fingers, or go cross-eyed. Where it becomes troubling is when it joins with sexual fantasies and/or pornography. Then it can even become compulsive and addictive.

By focusing too much on masturbation—by making it sound like the forbidden fruit—you can actually push your child to become more dependent on it. It's fairly safe to assume that most boys, and very many girls, will occasionally masturbate. Research tells us that 90 percent of adolescent boys masturbate—and the other 10 percent are liars! For boys in particular, a physiological pressure builds up during the sperm-making process. One way or another, that sperm is going to come out.

Some girls discover that touching themselves can be pleasurable. Some parents may see this as sin, others as a morally neutral activity, provided it is not accompanied by sinful activity (engaging in explicit fantasies or using pornography).

It's not our desire to advocate one position over the other. Be careful, however, about jumping to conclusions! One mother we know walked into the bathroom when her son was in the shower. Her son didn't see her come in, and though she had the door open only for a moment, she believed he had been masturbating.

Parents often panic when they see kids begin touching themselves around the crotch area. What they forget, however, is that the penis and the vagina are body parts that, like all body parts, sometimes get an itch or a rash. Don't always assume that if your child is fishing around down there, it's masturbation, especially at this age. Moms, boys often "adjust themselves," and dads, girls need to adjust their pads. These are pubescent kids, not adolescent kids, and for many of them, the hormones haven't yet kicked in. In the early puberty years, most kids are still more interested in playing in the mud or tying ribbons around the dog's neck than in relieving sexual tension. Your kid could be doing all kinds of things down there, things more similar to picking their nose than to fantasizing about sex.

In fact, what looks like masturbation could be any of several things:

- Innocent self-exploration: Getting used to pubic hair, growing genitals, pads for menstruation.
- Irritation: Ranging from irritation from such things as bubble bath or urine to irritation from an infection.

It might sound crazy to talk about taking masturbation "in stride," but try to find casual ways to discuss it. Try asking, "You've got your hands in your pants—what's up?"

If you're already connected with your kid, she's not going to say, "Mom!"

Ultimately, you and your spouse have to decide on your values regarding masturbation. Where do the two of you stand? If you attach religious values to it, then do your research. Talk with your pastor. Know why you believe what you believe before you talk with your child, because the tone of your voice will state your values even if your words do not. Kids' hands are going to be there for all sorts of reasons—most of them not sexual—so what are you going to say about it when it's still innocent? Please, talk about it *before* it becomes a sexual issue. Then pray for the right time and the words to talk about it in a way that keeps communication open, and encourage your kids to consider more productive ways to release that energy: sports, creative arts, and the like.

In short, don't ignore the m-word, but don't make it a bigger issue than it is.

Take a Step Back

Admittedly, these are all difficult issues. None of us relish the idea of talking about erections, wet dreams, and masturbation with our children. But you know what? The vast majority of pubescents—probably over 90 percent in our experience—are left to flounder through these realities on their own. And that's really sad.

One of the best gifts you can give your child is not a new car on their sixteenth birthday. It's not even the $50,000 you saved up for their college education. If you can provide your son or daughter with a healthy understanding of sex, clear and accurate information about their sexual maturation, and values to guide them into marriage—well, frankly, we can't imagine a much better gift than that, short of a relationship with God.

Take the time; fight through the embarrassment. Give your children an inheritance that they will be able to treasure for the rest of their lives.

Chapter 11

Home Plate—The Big "It"

Talking to Your Pubescent Child about Sexual Intercourse

I (Kathy) was preparing pork chops for dinner when the phone rang. In addition to balancing plates and checking to make sure the pork chops wouldn't burn, I picked up the receiver with greasy hands.

"Hello, Mrs. Bell?" asked a female voice.

Grrrrrr. Sounded like a telemarketer. But since I once worked in telemarketing, I do my best to turn them down gently. "Yes," I replied in a forced, polite tone.

"Hi, this is Julia—from class today. I need to ask you a question. Do you mind?"

I looked at the kitchen chaos, the cooking dishes strewn over the counter, the sizzling pork chops, the seasoning bottles left opened . . .

"I'm getting dinner on the table," I replied, "but I have a few minutes."

I mentally reviewed my classes that day, trying to match the name Julia to a face. *Julia. Julia. Which one was Julia?*

"Mrs. Bell, I just had sex with my boyfriend," Julia said. "The white stuff coming out of me—is that something to worry about?"

I set down the plates, my rush to get dinner on the table suddenly seeming very insignificant.

Julia's boyfriend was in high school, six years older than she was. With that age discrepancy, you could legitimately call him a sexual predator. As a seventh grader, Julia had no clue as to what she was participating in. She mistakenly believed that her need to be loved could be fulfilled by a naked embrace with a much older boy.

If it weren't so tragic, the conversation that followed would almost have been comic. After talking with one of her girlfriends, Julia had come to the conclusion that the "white stuff" was "probably" sperm. Even so, she seemed amazingly unconcerned about the possibility of becoming pregnant or of getting an STD. She had focused exclusively on that strange, white substance seeping out of her body; *that* was what frightened her. Frankly, the sperm coming *out* of Julia was the least of her concerns. The sperm that still remained inside, the possible STD that even now might be gaining a foothold in her body, the spiritual damage of being taken advantage of sexually—these were all serious concerns to which Julia remained shockingly ignorant.

Unfortunately, Julia's ignorance about the mechanics and risks of sexual intercourse—not to mention about her own body—is not uncommon. The mathematical equation for sex among many young kids goes something like this:

$$guy + girl \times sex = (chance \text{ to get pregnant}) \div (it \text{ won't happen to me})$$

While most kids get the big picture, the specifics of sexual intercourse and its aftermath are often so inaccurate that one wonders exactly what is taught in general anatomy and reproductive science class. Kids may hear STD and pregnancy statistics spouted from the front of the class, but if nothing has happened to their sexually active friends, those statistics simply remain numbers scribbled on a chalkboard.

If it hasn't happened to Jenny and Ian, who I know are having sex, why would it happen to me?

Julia's single mother felt deeply concerned about her daughter's behavior, but though she seemed ready to do what she could to help, unfortunately, she had little time for her daughter at home. Consequently, Julia was often left alone. This young girl's need to be loved outweighed any busy mom's expectations of her.

Am I Good Enough to Be Loved?

Julia's attempt to fill her heart by activating her genitals betrays how most pubescent kids feel far more interested in feelings than in sexual ecstasy. Kids this age simply are not ready for sex, and most of them know it. That's why they concern themselves less with the mechanics of intercourse than with questions of the heart:

- How will I know when I've fallen in love, and how do you stay in love?
- Why do girls talk about marriage so soon?
- Why doesn't he call me anymore?

- Will a boy break up with me if I don't let him slip his hand under my shirt?

Pubescent kids have little interest in figuring out sexual technique or positions; they want to know that they are desirable to the opposite sex and that the future marriage they dream about will not end up in divorce. Those pubescent kids who do become sexually active often do so because they believe it's expected of them, because they don't want to miss out on all the fun they perceive others as having, and because they have no other voices to listen to than those of the world, telling them that sexual activity, even at a young age, is a "normal" rite of life.

One girl wrote to me (Kathy) a heartrending letter: "When you don't fit in," she began, "but want desperately to hang out with everybody who seems to be having fun, you let them define who you are, rather than define it yourself. When you hear over and over again that sex is what 'everybody's doing,' you begin to believe it." In other words, she's saying, "Sex is the price you're willing to pay to fit in."

Unfortunately, this girl had her heart cruelly broken when she finally gave in to her boyfriend at a party. She really liked this boy, and he had been pressuring her for some time to have sex. Since most of her friends assumed she was having sex anyway, she finally decided, "Why not?"

Well, she found out "why not" shortly thereafter. In a tale that won't surprise any adult, the sex that followed was anything but fun, and it eventually lowered, rather than raised, her popularity. Almost as soon as her boyfriend had zipped up his pants, he began spreading obscene rumors and inventing cruel names to describe this soon-to-be heartbroken girl.

What can *you* do to stand against the tide of your child's sexual seduction? Remember, you are *still* your child's greatest influence. Most sexually active pubescents and adolescents have one thing in common: Busy parents. Distracted parents. Overwhelmed parents.

Protecting your child is all about that parent-child relationship, remaining heavily involved in your child's life, and preserving your child's sense of belonging at home. As your child grows, you will need to express your love differently to match her growing independence. But it is still your affirmation that answers your pubescent child's question, "Am I lovable?" Your daughter's best defense against a sexual predator— an older boy—is a caring and involved father. Your son's best defense against a wily seductress is a great relationship with his mom.

In other words, don't make the mistake so many educators make: giving kids more technical information than they need or want and hoping they manage premature sexual relationships without *too* much trauma. Instead, focus on meeting their emotional needs, reinforce their desire to be abstinent until marriage, and affirm their sense of belonging.

Why Sexual Education *Must* Be Addressed at Home

Steve Parsons, a youth pastor in Woodinville, Washington, was surfing through TV channels one evening when he noticed that one of the women on a particular program seemed awfully familiar. It wasn't a show that Steve would normally watch, but the young woman had been in his youth group years before—and that stopped Steve short.

The series was called *Temptation Island* and had a worldly premise: A "reality" TV show in which four unmarried couples are brought to a tropical island to have their fidelity tested by thirteen men and thirteen women. Steve's former youth group girl was one of the thirteen women "tempting" the guys away from their partners.

Dropping your kid off at church every Wednesday night will not guarantee that they'll adopt the church's values. Sexual temptation is a tremendous force, and being a Christian doesn't exempt your kid from it any more than marriage exempts you from infidelity. Some kids go to youth group, wear their Christian fish T-shirts, carry their Bibles, perform in the church Christmas or Easter play, attend summer camp— and then have sex with each other during the weekend.

One of our dentists has a plaque on his office wall that reads: "The six most dangerous words in the world: *I think it will go away*." It's one thing to polish those ivories on the outside and make them look nice, and it's another thing entirely to take that little pick and shovel and go to work on something you may not be able to see or even feel. But it's necessary. Does it feel good? No. Is it fun to think about bleeding and spitting into the bowl? Not really. But when your dentist says, "Hey, we need to reschedule an appointment to take care of what we found today," you pay attention, even though it is human nature to look the other way.

Some parents believe sending their kid to a Christian school or dragging them along to church inoculates them against sexual experimentation. As good as some Christian schools are, and as much as we believe in them, godly values still have to be internalized. Your kid has to be convinced he *wants* to be different than the crowd and save himself for marriage.

This type of persuasion has to be initiated and reinforced at home. Complementary messages at school and church provide helpful aides, *but they are not substitutes for your involvement*. The sense of belonging that fortifies the choice to become abstinent comes from home.

Now that we have stressed the importance of your child's emotional needs during puberty (and they really *are* critical), let's get into the actual mechanics of talking about sex with your pubescent child.

Tell It Like It Is

Parents often ask, "Exactly how do you tell your child what intercourse is? How do you actually say that the penis goes into the vagina?" Since we're not accustomed to talking about these things in explicit terms, kids usually get the message in more roundabout ways.

We've heard some hilarious stories.

"You know how a flashlight goes into a cave," one girl's older sister told her, "and that's how you see?"

The younger sister nodded.

"Well," she said, "it's kind of like that."

The younger sister thought for a moment. Finally, she said, "Are you saying that . . ." as she made hand motions.

"Yup," the older sister replied.

Or this:

"Remember the time we drove by that farm and we saw that one cow climbing up on the back of that other cow?"

"Ewwww. You mean they do that?"

"Uh-huh."

"Why would Mom let him? After all, Dad's a little heavy . . ."

Here's the danger of the indirect approach: not only are your children likely to get *wrong* information; they are just as likely to get *immoral* information. If they can't get their questions answered at home, they'll get them answered elsewhere, and when that happens, your ability to place sexual activity within the framework of your values has evaporated.

Kids want to know about their changing bodies. As parents, we fear that any mention of the word *sex* will leave them groping for each other, but the reality is that for most of these kids, sexual intercourse is simply a Lego piece to click into the larger context of understanding the world. Sex, when you come right down to it for young pubescent kids, sounds just plain gross.

Here are some guidelines to help you keep your discussion age-appropriate.

Focus on biology. When kids think about birth, they don't imagine that women go through agonizing hours of contractions or even occasionally rip and require episiotomies. They just think about what they know: the mystique and wonder of a beautiful baby coming out.

And that's okay.

Similarly, as we've mentioned, you can't expect a fifth grader to fully comprehend the act of sexual intercourse. In early puberty, let kids develop their own mental picture of what sex is, based on your conversations about the body parts and how babies are made. Let them sit with the pieces they can hold and process them in the innocence of the imagination God gave them until they're ready to open themselves further.

Pubescents don't need blow-by-blow descriptions of sexual positions, conversations about the "G" spot, or descriptions about what a woman sounds like in the throes of orgasm. In your desire to properly educate them, don't destroy their God-given modesty and innocence. It's okay at this stage in their development to be general and to leave certain specifics out of your conversation.

First and foremost, when talking about sexual intercourse, talk about the *biology* behind it. People need to understand that despite all the press our genitalia get, they're just body parts. Our society idolizes intercourse, forgetting that many pubescent kids are going to express more interest in how babies get made.

"Won't talking about it make them want to do it sooner?" some parents ask. It all depends on where you're coming from. Remember, we're not talking about bringing up clitoral stimulation, oral sex, and multiple orgasms! When talking to pubescents, keep the focus of the conversation where it belongs: on physiology and how babies are formed.

Respect for sex is caught, not just taught. "Make sure you tell them sex is sacred. Make sure they understand that sex is holy," parents often tell us when they find out one of us will be speaking to their children. What we want to tell those parents in return is, "Make sure *you* live a life that communicates that sex is sacred. Make sure *you* treat sex as holy."

We know of one mom who had become sexually active at the age of sixteen. She felt motivated to talk with her daughter about sex because no one had talked with her, and she believed that if she communicated to her daughter how special a woman's sexuality is, she could help her daughter avoid what she had gone through.

More relationship, less Twister. Because words do not adequately describe sex, our culture often resorts to titillation and absurdity. We print magazine articles with titles like, "Twenty-five Things You Can Lick to Get the Best Sex Tonight" or "Five Places You Can Touch That Will Have Him Begging for More."

Such articles turn sex into an undercover Twister game. In fact, good sex between a husband and wife is not about ability or intensity as much as it is about loving each other. Sure, there's a place to discuss sexual skills. Dr. Leman has even written an entire book on the subject *(Sheet Music)*. But sexual intimacy between a husband and wife is a very *spiritual* exercise, one of God's mysteries, and some things go on in the spiritual realm during sex that we cannot comprehend. Don't be afraid to have conversations that reach beyond your own knowledge into the mysterious realm of the sacred.

We say this because in today's mind, sex is 100 percent physical and 0 percent spiritual. If we don't balance this—by stressing the spiritual connection, the importance of relationship, how what we do *outside* the bedroom influences what happens *inside* the bedroom (see Dr. Leman's book *Sex Begins in the Kitchen*)—then our children won't receive an accurate depiction of the place of sex within marriage.

Good sex really *does* begin in the kitchen; it is part of a larger relationship and encompasses the whole person. That makes it dishonest for us to describe sex apart from that relationship.

Tell it like it is. When parents ask, "How do you tell kids the penis goes into the vagina?" what they're really asking is, "Is there any way to say it in different terms that will make it less embarrassing for me?"

The answer to that question is a resounding "No."

Talking about the penis going into the vagina isn't easy, simply because it's not something we talk about often or well. And quite frequently, the opportunity to begin such a discussion may come from unpleasant circumstances.

My (Kathy's) daughter Amy was in kindergarten when she first asked about sex. At the time, we lived in an inner-city neighborhood near the local school, where for a few weeks a rapist was at large. Parents in the neighborhood did not let kids out by themselves because this man committed his crimes almost daily. Amy had heard the word "rapist" numerous times, and one day she asked what it meant.

"A man that hurts women," I said.

"No, Momma," she said, "I want to know more."

"A man who hurts women in their private area," I added.

Finally, after a few weeks, she asked, "Momma, what is sex?"

I looked at her.

"I heard it because of the rapist," she said.

"Well," I replied, "sex is something God intended to happen between a husband and wife. It's something very special that married people do together. But this rapist is using sex to hurt women."

"Mommy," Amy replied, looking at me with that knowing look, "Mommy, I *know* it has something to do with a man and his body down there. And I know it has something to do with a woman and her body down there. And I know it has something to do with people being naked. And I know it has something to do with people being married. I just don't know how it gets all together."

When I told her, she said the same thing that John had said in the field with the cows: "Yuck! Gross! I knew it was something like that."

Once kids know the body parts and the basic formula for pregnancy, they usually don't ask a bunch of questions about technique. Which is how it should be. Even the sight of a very passionate kiss is usually too much for pubescent kids. They tend to respond with "Gross!" and leave it at that.

Sperm and Egg

Materials: One grain of salt or sugar, one small head of broccoli.

Objective: To discover the shapes of the female egg and male sperm.

Pick one grain of salt or sugar and place it on the table. Next, cut the tips off the broccoli. The grain is like the female's egg and the little pieces of broccoli are like the millions of sperm from a man. It is not to scale, but it gives an idea of the shape of each. Now pick one set, one "egg" and one "sperm." This is how you and your child came to be! Tell them, "You won the race! You are one in a million—literally! You are here for a reason!"

Keep in mind that it won't be as uncomfortable for you to say, "The husband puts his penis inside the wife's vagina," if you taught your children the proper names for these body parts early on. If you referred to your boy's penis as "his thing," or your daughter's vagina as "that area down there," then you will feel more uncomfortable once they get older and start asking questions about sex because you've never really even talked about the genitals.

In short, start with the biology of sexuality, model a healthy sexual relationship with your spouse, don't forget to stress the relational and spiritual connection of sex, allow certain details to remain unstated, and use specific names—tell it like it is. Nine times out of ten, after you sweat through this process, you're still going to hear a pubescent say, "Oh, that's so gross!"

Don't worry; when you hear that, take it as a badge of honor. You've done your job!

How Would You Respond to These Statements about Sexual Intercourse?

Note: these are all actual questions from children fifth grade and up.

What is sex?	What does it feel like?
Is it wrong to have sex?	Can you not have sex?
Do people like sex?	Why do people have sex?
Do you have to have sex?	Have you had sex?
What is a virgin?	Is it okay to touch someone?
What is an orgasm?	Were you a virgin?

Chapter 12

Wonka Sex—Building a Bridge to Adolescence

Talking to Your Child about Abstinence

Though most pubescents still think of sex as "gross," the time is rapidly approaching when their attitude will change in a very dramatic and intense way. If you do your job with them as pubescents, the bridge into adolescence will seem natural and unforced. You've kept the communication highway in good repair. You're relatively comfortable talking about the body parts because you've done it. They've learned that you're a knowledgeable and helpful source of accurate information. If all this is true, helping them internalize sexual purity will seem but a natural and small step forward.

How do you know when it's time to cross the bridge into adolescence? Well, it's a judgment call. One dad noticed a change in his twelve-year-old son when an ad featuring a bikini-clad woman came on the air. Six months earlier, this boy would have shouted, "Sick!" Now, the dad noticed, his son's eyes remained glued to the television set.

The next day they went for a drive and had a good talk.

It'll be like that for you. You start to notice that your child's attitudes are changing and the hormones are kicking it up a gear. Such signals tell you that you need to provide more than information and biology; it's time to talk specifically about future decision making.

Since Dr. Leman has dealt with parenting adolescents in another book *(Adolescence Isn't Terminal: It Just Feels Like It!)*, we don't want to go into too much detail here. However, we do think it's appropriate and necessary to talk about the bridge into adolescence and how to begin talking about sexual abstinence to kids who, far from thinking sex is gross, view sex as the most exciting present in the world, a present they just can't wait to open.

Is It or Isn't It?

"When I was younger," said Kate—referring to a time in the fifth grade—"oral sex was kind of a slutty thing to do. But now, it's like everyone's at least having oral sex. Freshmen [in high school, ninth graders] might wait up to a year, but sophomores wait, at most, a couple of months."

"It's like an added base," Lara adds.

"Like shortstop or something," says Lynn, who is a virgin.[1]

This recounting of an actual conversation between girls, captured in *U.S. News and World Report,* tells us that in the minds of today's kids, the definition of *virgin* has been lowered past the floor of the Grand Canyon. Some girls believe they're still virgins as long as a penis has never penetrated their vaginas, even though they may have engaged in oral sex with the entire basketball team. Other kids may engage in all kinds of sexual activity, including heavy petting while being naked together, but as long as they stop short of intercourse, they rationalize, "We were just fooling around. We're not sexually active."

While percentages are down slightly for the number of adolescent kids engaging in intercourse, the number of those who don't call oral sex "sex" has greatly increased. Claude Allen, deputy secretary for the Department of Health and Human Services, said, "When we ask young people, 'Have you engaged in sexual activity?' we often hear, 'Well, what do you mean by that?'"[2]

We're certain that this shift in mentality was not helped by a certain high-ranking official who became well known for his comment that he did not have sex "with that woman," when we know for sure "that woman" serviced him orally.

What exactly is sex? It's imperative in today's environment that we define this word, since all too many kids (and, unfortunately, even some educators) are redefining it. For our purposes, *sex is any activity in which body parts normally clothed by a bathing suit are touched, massaged, played with, kissed, or sucked*. Such activities may not constitute sexual intercourse, but they certainly comprise sexual activity.

Many Christian youth today are hearing the message that they're supposed to abstain from sex before marriage. But they're taking the lesson to its pharisaical conclusion, trying to get away with all sorts of other sexual behavior without "going all the way." Or they may justify intercourse by saying, "It's okay because we both love each other, we're both

Christians, and we're going to spend the rest of our lives together anyway." In other words, parents, it's not enough to emphasize *abstinence;* we must emphasize *purity*.

Any sexual activity outside of marriage comes with a heavy price tag. Reputations can be ruined, health can be devastated, integrity can be compromised, and hearts can be broken, all without engaging in a single act of sexual intercourse. A lot of sins appear to be fun at first, but they pull an entire train of problems behind them. Take it a step further, and the consequences become even more severe. The problem with herpes simplex II, HIV, or an out-of-wedlock pregnancy is that they all end up being "gifts" that "keep on giving."

Whatever today's kids choose to call it, sexual activity outside of marriage is physically, emotionally, psychologically, and spiritually damaging.

Liar, Liar, Pants on Fire!

As soon as your child hits adolescence, she may become obsessed with romance. How else to explain the unprecedented popularity of the new reality dating shows? It doesn't take much of a grip on reality to know that these TV shows are anything but real.

"Oh boy, now there's what love is all about!" I (Dr. Leman) joked when I walked into the living room the other night and found my oldest daughter, Holly, watching *The Bachelorette* with Hannah. How often does a woman have twenty men vying for her affection, while every minute of their conversation is recorded and watched by 20 million people?

Fortunately, our daughters know the difference; they've seen their parents, who have been married for thirty-six years.

Our children are being lied to almost every day. They're being given a vision that is not only untrue; it's harmful and misleading. It is our job as parents to set the record straight.

Do you remember hearing the phrase "You can't believe everything you hear" repeated by parents, friends, and teachers growing up? That's a message worth passing on. The sooner our children realize that they can't trust everything they hear on TV or read in a book, newspaper, or magazine, the better.

All sorts of lies are flying around out there, and it's good to point these out to kids.

"Sex is safe if you wear a condom." For years, condoms have been trumpeted as the answer to society's sexual ills. But notice, condom manufacturers don't use "safe sex" in their advertising anymore. Now it's "safer sex." If you wear a condom, you have *less* dangerous sex, but it's still dangerous sex. Even condom manufacturers won't tell you they're foolproof. The fact is, you can still get STDs with a condom.

"I used to think all we had to do was dump condoms in the schools and be done with it," says Dr. Patricia Sulak, an obstetrician-gynecologist and a professor at Texas A&M University's College of Medicine. "But after reviewing the data, I've had to do a 180 on kids and sex." An STD such as human papillomavirus, which is linked to cervical cancer, is not only transmitted through skin-to-skin contact of the genitals but also of the area around them. Which means there is no such thing as safe sex outside of a faithfully monogamous marriage.[3]

"Sex is a wonderful, euphoric, blissful experience." Well, sex *can* be all of that, but sex also has the potential to be one of the most painful and heartbreaking acts two people ever commit together.

Let's face it, good sex takes a certain amount of skill. When it comes to sex, women are like crockpots; men are like microwaves. To be a good lover, you need to have the discipline to take time, focus on *her,* and develop the patience to go against your natural instincts to rush through everything. These are all qualities that the vast majority of average teenage guys can't even spell, let alone practice.

That's why there's no worse lover than a horny teenage guy who drops his load in 6.7 seconds and then rushes out to tell his friends about the mind-blowing experience he just had. The young woman, who wants to feel loved, suddenly discovers she was nothing more to him than a sexual receptacle. More often than not, teen sex is a painful, guilt-producing, relationship-destroying activity.

Even sex among seemingly sensitive teens tends to be disappointing when all is said and done. Lucian had planned to remain a virgin until his wedding night—that is, until the opportunity "came along" one night and he decided to compromise on his earlier commitment. As usually happens in such cases, the sex was over quickly, without the intimacy or romance that Lucian expected. No fireworks went off; the relationship didn't rise to a new level. There was just a somewhat embarrassing cleanup and then an awkward, "What's next?" "Emotionally, it felt really awkward," said Lucian. "It was not what I expected it to be."[4]

Now, having said that, we think it's entirely appropriate to also point out to your kids that when a married couple has the security of a lifelong commitment—and the time to really practice and get to know each other's likes and dislikes and favorite spots and personal preferences—well, then, sex is absolutely magnificent! Nothing on this earth is like it. But two rushed, hurried, and unmarried teens won't have this type of experience.

"You can't get pregnant the first time you have sex." It's hard to believe how naïve some kids can be. The thought that you can't get pregnant the first time you have sexual intercourse is bewilderingly common; so common, in fact, that it needs to be addressed directly and dispelled.

Try putting it this way: "Let's say a teacher lines up six twelve-year-olds five feet in front of a basketball hoop. None of them have ever played basketball. Each kid is given one shot—their very first attempt at a half free throw. Do you think it's possible for any of them to make a basket?"

"Of course!" the kids will answer.

"But they've never shot a basketball!"

"That doesn't matter. It's only five feet, and it's not that hard."

"In the same way, a couple can easily get pregnant the very first time they have sexual intercourse. Conception is a mechanical process; if a woman gets semen inside her body, that process is set in motion. She's *designed* to get pregnant, and the body won't distinguish between this being her first or her millionth time of having sex.

"The fact is, you can get pregnant without even having sexual intercourse if semen is released close enough to the opening of the vagina. That's right; if a girl is naked with her partner, and the boy ejaculates, and some of that ejaculate gets near the opening of the girl's vagina, it's possible for her to become pregnant.

"If you have sex, odds are that eventually you will get pregnant—maybe not the first time, though that is certainly possible, but eventually it's going to happen."

It might be helpful to point out that most teen pregnancies occur within the first six months of sexual activity.[5]

"Sex is just between two people." If you become pregnant at fifteen, sex suddenly becomes a *lot* of people's business. If there's a conception, parents and grandparents have to step in. If you're a young, unwed mother on state welfare, you become a concern of taxpayers. Being a child without two parents becomes a concern for that child, and certainly if he or she is aborted, that child pays the ultimate price of never experiencing life.

177

In fact, we know of one physician, Dr. Mary Adam, who used to routinely ask her young patients, "How many sexual partners have you had? How many do you expect to have by the time you graduate from high school?" Her purpose in asking this was to get the young girls thinking about *cumulative* risk. Sex isn't just between two people, particularly if either partner has had previous sexual relationships.

While becoming pregnant out of wedlock sends ripples through a community, even if you don't become pregnant, the effects of premarital sex follow you through life. You're giving away something you can never get back, to a boy who may not even remember your name in another fifteen years. I (Dr. Leman) wish I could record some of the conversations I have had in the counseling room—how women fight against mental comparisons, sexual flashbacks, and their lack of sexual freedom within marriage. It hurts them terribly when they realize that they gave themselves more freely to a boyfriend who is now off raising some other woman's children than they've ever been able to give themselves to their husbands, who love them, support them, and are committed to them.

Our brains do not have efficient delete buttons. We tend to remember most of what happens in our life, especially the most significant events, and there aren't many experiences in life more profound than sexual ones. Fifteen years from now, when your daughter has been married for five years, is she really going to want to have flashbacks of sleeping with Daniel . . . and Stan . . . and Chris . . . as she tries to enjoy her husband in bed?

Truth You Can Count On

The best way to combat lies is with the truth. We need to refute today's propaganda with wisdom that we know is true:

God's laws are perfect. "How can a young man keep his way pure?" the psalmist asks in Psalm 119:9, a wonderful picture of the beauty of God's law. "By living according to your word."

We need to explain to our kids that sex was God's idea. He thought it up, he created it, and then he designed our bodies to experience it. He put a sexual organ inside the woman, the clitoris, that has just *one* function—sexual pleasure. He put more nerve endings on the end of a man's penis than anywhere else on the body, with the exception of the taste buds.

And then he told us when and how to experience sex: within the bounds of a committed, lifelong marriage. He knows that is where sex works best.

It's really very simple: doesn't it make sense to read the directions written by the one who designed the experience? God's ways really are the best, steering us away from the pain of our own foolish paths.

Sex is not bad; sex is great! Please, let's *not* communicate that sex is bad; sex is great! If we turn sex into something bad or naughty, we impugn one of God's most wonderful gifts. Far from condemning our sexuality, the Bible celebrates it. The Song of Songs is a poem of erotic dialogue between a man and his beloved new bride, so explicit it makes many blush. You won't find a single biblical book devoted to prayer, charity, or handling money. But there *is* one book of the Bible devoted exclusively to sex.

It's healthy for kids to know that their parents enjoy sexual intimacy. Not that we should ever flaunt it or expose them to it explicitly; that would be wrong. But it's a positive thing to model the purity of sexual desire within marriage. When a girl sees her mom shove her dad's hands away from her when he comes up behind her as she's doing the dishes, the mom saying, "Oh, honey, you dirty old man!" that tells the daughter that sex is a lecherous act that women need to resist. If, on the other hand, she sees her mom drop what she's doing, turn around, and plant a big kiss on her husband's lips, that's sending a very positive, sex-affirming message.

You can wait. I (Dr. Leman) gave Hannah a little gold medallion, along with a note comparing the purity of the gold to that of her life and offering a prayer that she would keep herself pure until marriage, overcoming all the inevitable impulses and temptations along the way.

I gave that medallion to Hannah without a chain because I wanted to see what she would do with it. Would she put it in a drawer and forget about it? Would she leave it by her nightstand, until it fell down under her bed, only to be recovered when she cleaned out her room for college? Or would she—and this was my hope—take the initiative and wear it around her neck?

I knew it would have to be her decision.

By two o'clock that afternoon, I was one pleased papa. Hannah had found a chain, put the medallion on it, and was wearing it around her neck.

Throughout life we have all kinds of impulses. We teach toddlers not to respond with anger by hitting, not to respond to frustration by throwing a tantrum, and not to seek attention by screaming. We hope that by the time they become pubescents, our children have learned to tame these primitive reactions.

Handling sexual impulses is simply the next stage in their development. It is no more unrealistic to ask them to refrain from sexual activity than it is to teach them that they can't slug a brother or sister just because they feel like it. Having them sign an abstinence pledge acknowledges this on paper and serves as a reminder that the human will *can* temper the desires.

The truth is, your son or daughter can wait for sex. Sande and I waited for marriage to have sex. Your kids can, too.

Everybody isn't doing it. For years I (Dr. Leman) helped run the residence halls at the University of Arizona. I remember reading statistics then of how many kids were hopping into the sack with each other. *Where are all these statistics coming from?* I thought. Since I lived with them, I knew that most of the kids in our halls—those I talked to daily—weren't dating. In fact, only about one out of ten of them dated regularly. Most all of them spent Friday nights sitting at home, looking at each other and trying to find something to do.

When you hear statistics that say a certain percentage of kids have had sex by the age of twenty, keep in mind that a single act of sex will elicit a "yes" answer. A person who is twenty has lived approximately 175,000 hours. If they've had sex once, they've spent only 1 out of 175,000 hours having sex, but they would still answer yes to whether they've had sex, and many researchers would classify them as "sexually active." Even if they've had sex ten times, you're still talking about maybe 15 hours out of the 175,000 hours they've lived.

The notion that every teenager is spending hours every weekend exploring the flesh of another person is simply not true. Many who *have* had sex have made subsequent commitments to refrain from any further sexual activity until after they are married. Hundreds of students, from all social groups, at Shadle Park High School and other high schools around Spokane, Washington, for example, have pledged abstinence through a program called SPAM, the Spokane Peer Abstinence Movement. The pregnancy rate in the county is the lowest it's been since 1978, and health officials partly credit abstinence education such as SPAM, which was started after a couple of teenage girls talked to teachers about their regrets over having sex.

"It is so cool to be a virgin at Shadle Park High School now," said one student. SPAM's success is due largely to the fact that many of the "instructors" for the human growth and development classes are high school juniors and seniors, people teens in middle school can relate to and can ask questions such as, "Will I make friends easily?" and "Is everyone in high school having sex?"[6]

Caution Signs

Remember when we talked about the danger of toxic shock for a young girl using a tampon? The warm temperature, combined with the blood, the moistness of the girl's body, and the superabsorbent material of the tampon, produce a near perfect environment for bacteria to grow.

In the same way, the wrong mix of social factors can create a more susceptible environment for social and relational failure. Let's look at two of the most common caution signs.

Uninvolved parents. Parents and policy makers used to be concerned about kids stealing away after school to have sex. It turns out that the bigger risk is now at home: kids having sex while their parents watch TV or do the laundry in the next room!

A nationwide poll tracked the sexual activity of 8,000 teens, ages twelve to sixteen, since 1997. It showed that, of the 664 who first had sex between 1999 and 2000, "56 percent ... say they've had sex at home—while their parents were in the house."[7] Of those teens who admitted having sex at home, 70 percent had sex between 6:00 P.M. and 7:00 A.M.; nearly half of that number was between 10:00 P.M. and 7:00 A.M.[8]

This isn't to say that you should start wandering through the living room every five minutes to ask if your daughter's friends want popcorn for the video they're watching. But it does mean you don't leave an adolescent boy and girl undisturbed behind a locked door. It's not safe.

If your children are engaged in appropriate activities, there's no reason for absolute privacy. We're not saying you should be standing in the same room all the time, listening to every giggle and nugget of conversation. But you know what? They should be aware that you could show up at *any* time.

Also, help your child set a healthy schedule. Kids don't need to be out late "just hanging out." Their natural inhibitions go down steadily every hour after their bedtime.

Be involved. Establish a healthy routine and know what's going on in your kid's life.

Inhibition-reducing substances. A very offensive "shock jock" is building a national audience by telling men "how to get more [sex] for less money." His number one piece of advice: fill the woman with alcohol.

In a survey sponsored by the Kaiser Family Foundation, "more than a third of sexually active teens and young adults ... admit that alcohol and drugs have influenced their decisions about sex. Nearly a quarter say they have had unprotected sex while under the influence."[9] Drinking and driving have always been a concern; now drinking and having sex are proving a dangerous mix, as well.

Our daughters and sons need to know that alcohol and "social" drugs reduce our natural, God-given inhibitions. Drinking is never a good idea on a date.

Many a conscientious young teen has woken up with a hangover, a new STD, and a heart full of regret. Beer ads show young people having a good time, laughing, and partying; they never show how much pain many feel the next morning. It's our job to point that one out.

Wonka Sex

Before me (Kathy) sat a group of hardened juvenile delinquents, one step away from lockup. Many of the girls wouldn't even make eye contact with me; it was a miracle, I was told, that many of them had even showed up. The majority of their offenses were gang related, along with other forms of physical aggression. And, yes, they were sexually active. Once they knew I was there to talk about sex, their questions began to fly.

"When the woman's [cervical] mucus is like this [making finger motions], can she get pregnant?"

"If I've got my chlamydia back, does that mean I need more antibiotics?"

My mind spun. *I'm here to teach abstinence?!* I thought.

About that time an idea hit.

Unless teens experience what needs to be learned, they will have a hard time understanding intangible concepts. It doesn't make sense to them when you say sex is a great gift but you can get diseases from it. You're telling them to wait in a world that tells them not to wait, and that was the problem I faced every time I went into classrooms.

Frankly, movies can be a big hurdle to overcome. What kids feel when they look up at the big screen and watch the latest Hollywood couple "falling in love," they accept as truth, and that feeling becomes the principle by which they make future decisions. Statistics seem dead; what they watch on the silver screen comes alive in a way that a textbook never can. Young kids rarely question what they see in a two-hour movie; the emotions they experience become their reality.

Rather than fighting this, I've learned to use it. Many of my workshops utilize movie clips. For one talk, I prayed about a movie clip I could use to describe the wonders of healthy sex. God brought to mind an illustration that I've used ever since.

In the movie *Willie Wonka and the Chocolate Factory,* five families win the rare opportunity to tour the mysterious, magical chocolate factory. Toward the beginning of their tour, Willie Wonka leads them down a narrowing hallway toward an incredibly small door.

"My dear friends," says Willie Wonka, "you are now about to enter the nerve center of the entire Wonka factory. Inside of this room, all of my dreams become realities." He taps in the right combination, and the door opens to an enormous, magnificent room filled with novelties and confections, a room bursting with color, waterfalls and rivers flowing chocolate, and lollipops like flowers. Speechless, the lucky winners enter; all their senses are attuned to the room around them.

Saving yourself for only *one* person in marriage is like that long, narrow hallway. It appears to be a dead end, so incredibly narrow-minded and out of touch with the "real world," something you could never fit through. But when the pastor at a marriage gives the blessing, something unseen happens in the spiritual realm. The creator of this room, marriage, is *the* Creator—God himself—and with the right combination of grace, time, respect, and love, the married couple enters a spiritual room intended for only the two of them. It's what I call Wonka sex— the best sex in the world.

In the 1994 study "Sex in America"—what *Time* magazine referred to as "probably the first truly scientific survey of who does what with whom in America and just how often they do it"[10]—the research team found that married couples have the best sex. "Once again contradicting the common view of marriage as dull and routine," the survey said, "the people who reported being the most physically pleased and emotionally satisfied were the married couples."[11]And, as *Time* magazine pointed out in its summary of the results, Christians have it good. "The women most likely to achieve orgasm each and every time (32 percent) are, believe it or not, conservative Protestants."[12]

"You're not going to read about this in *Redbook*," I told the kids. "We don't have words on this earth to adequately describe intimate, marital sex."

It's difficult for kids to admit the sexual pressure they feel in the later pubescent and early adolescent years. *Mom and Dad,* your kid might think, *I know that you're telling me that you don't want me to have sex, but right now the thought of having that guy wrap me in his arms feels like it fulfills something in me that you can't.* If you want to help your kids understand that marriage is the best place and time to have sex and that sex within marriage is worth waiting for, then you have to: (1) find a way to talk about sex so that they want to wait, and (2) give them incentive to do so.

Show It by Your Own Marriage

Does your marriage show your kids something worth waiting for? Your life is, after all, the greatest lesson your kid will ever receive. If you have things you want to communicate, you'd better be living them, because the most important point of reference for whether a kid decides to wait for marriage will be *your* marriage. Kids watch everything with their eyes, ears, and hearts, and they pay attention to the affection you show for each other and to how you talk about sex.

Quite frankly, your goal is simple: model the positive qualities of an intimate relationship in such a way that your kids will think, *I want what Mom and Dad have.* Otherwise, they're going to watch Kate Winslett and Leonardo DiCaprio in *Titanic* and think, *I want what* they *have.*

Hope and Dreams

People walk into marriage full of hope, with dreams of growing intimacy "so long as they both shall live."

"Adam, did you see what happens when two people have waited for one another?" Sharon said to her son in the parking lot after his summer-camp counselor's wedding. It had been such a joyous celebration, in which two people who had waited for one another could finally say before those who loved them, "I'm yours and you're mine." This event, powerful both emotionally and spiritually, was what God meant the joining of two persons to be.

Stress this to your children. Be frank and bold: "Honey, I want you to have a thrilling and fulfilling sexual life, and that means saving it for your spouse. Not only is this God's law; it's also common sense. The research is pretty clear: those who experience sex within marriage have the best sex out there. I want you to have Wonka sex, the best sex there is!"

Parents, your success in getting this message to your adolescent will depend on how you related to them as a pubescent. It hinges on whether you've taken the time to discuss the neck-up issues: acne, hair, and body hygiene. Things get more personal "neck to waist," and by the time trust is developed to discuss completely what needs to be discussed "waist down"—well, let's face it, you've either made it or you haven't. If you haven't, then you have to start all over again. Your success is based on being an involved parent who fights against the pull to become too busy. It depends on you having established a reputation as a knowledgeable and reliable authority. You've explained *how* it all works, so now they can trust you when you explain where and when it works best.

If you do this well, you will give your child a gift of inestimable value. If only you knew how few children receive a healthy explanation of sexuality. You don't need to be a millionaire to offer this priceless gift. Nor do you require a Ph.D. in child development. In fact, if you've made it this far, you already have all the basic information you need.

Now it's up to you. Will you give your child a healthy start?

Working with Your School and the Sex-Ed Teacher

S ex ed at school can be the sprig of parsley on whatever home-cooked meal you've already fixed for your kids. But don't fool yourself; one hour, five hours, or even fifteen hours in a sex-ed class will not suffice for your kid's complete education on sexuality. A sprig of parsley doesn't make a meal. It can serve as a finishing touch, but not as a substitute. Unfortunately, many times the school's sex-education program is a wilted, even rotting, sprig of parsley.

Consider the following guidelines as you evaluate and interact with your public school.

Define What Is Appropriate

Neither the penis nor the vagina are political; they are simply body parts. As long as accurate information is given, there really is no cause for concern over anatomy education delivered in an age-appropriate fashion. You have an elbow, a knee, and either a penis or a vagina. Properly labeling body parts should be a part of every school's curriculum and is nothing to get upset about.

It is the values attached to what we do with our genitals that get people fired up—and rightly so. As soon as values-laden information gets disseminated, parents have a right to be concerned. One teacher had to leave our district because she taught kids to call 1-900 sex lines to "take care of business." Parents who had asked to review her material discovered that her idea of abstinence education included advocating body massages and mutual masturbation.

Most everyone agrees that kids need education beyond anatomy, reproductive science, and basic hygiene. The question, however, is whether the school is the place to do that. Over the years we have noticed folks from both camps trying to stack the school board with members who will favor their preferred method of sex education. Indeed, sex education is often a key focal point of school-board decision making.

If we could have our way, we would move this information outside school hours to afternoons and Saturdays with parents invited, allowing board members to focus on the reasons why we send our children to school in the first place (reading, writing, math). In the real world, there *will* be some discussion about sexual practices during classroom hours; we believe, however, that it is inappropriate and a poor use of time to devote *entire semesters* to this subject matter.

Review the Teaching Materials and Curriculum

Most school districts know that their sex-education curriculum can become the basis for a lawsuit; consequently, they tend to be very forthcoming with information. You'll find that most schools will provide an outline of the sex-ed curriculum when asked. If you meet with resistance due to budget restrictions, offer to pay for the copies or ask to review the books and materials on the school premises.

We believe that every parent should review their child's curriculum. We want to know what our kids are hearing, because we want to know if the values he's receiving at home are being affirmed or challenged. We can't imagine handing over a pubescent child to a teacher we don't even know, any more than we can imagine letting a child of the same age wander alone at the mall for three or four hours.

Protect your children. Know what they're being assigned to read. Here are some good questions to ask:

1. Do you offer a parent class? (I first want to be taught what my child will be learning.) When will it be held?
2. What training have you had to teach this information?
3. What is the goal of each class?
4. What information will be taught to kids when separated by gender?
5. Are parents allowed in the classroom during class?
6. How does this program honor all lifestyle choices? (True "tolerance" recognizes that a teacher will not have enough time to honor all choices.)
7. Do you allow guest speakers? Are parents notified in advance of these?
8. How do you define *abstinence?*

9. How will you know if your program is successful?
10. Do our school's reading, math, and writing test scores afford us classroom time to do sex ed?

The bulk of information in public schools often comes from SIECUS (the education arm of Planned Parenthood) or Alan Gutmacher's Institute (the research arm of Planned Parenthood). Other materials might come from the U.S. government's Center for Disease Control and Prevention or the Department of Health and Human Services.

The Medical Institute for Sexual Health, on the other hand, does a great job of taking the gamut of information and promoting abstinence,[1] as does the Consortium of State Physicians Resource Councils.

Ideally, I (Kathy) would love all sex education to occur at home, but as you know, it continues overwhelmingly to be taught in the public school system. What I don't like is when the school presents its own values or has the opportunity to teach about intercourse before the parent does. At that point, they've circumvented the primary educator—you. I prefer teachers who are values-neutral, not advocating one position over another in the public-school setting, and providing information both for those kids who are sexually active *and* for those who aren't. You, the parent, can then talk with your child about your own values and about making choices, as well as about the choices others are making. I certainly am not neutral in my stance—nor should you be!

Parents should know about one challenge here: you can't always expect to be "buddy-buddy" with the school as you go through this process. You may have to ask some difficult questions and even apply some heat. In extreme circumstances, you might even consider legal action.

Talk with Other Parents

Reading the curriculum is a good *first* step, but it's not the final one. Some teachers may leave the most controversial part of their "education" out of print, saving those issues for their lectures. One of the best ways to find out about your school's curriculum is to sit down with parents whose kids have already gone through the class. Ask about the teacher's track record, any movies or videos that were shown, and anything that may not be mentioned in the curriculum. Also inquire about the methods employed. Were parents welcomed? Did their child hear anything that sounded unusual?

Inquire about Guest Speakers

Some districts do not permit guest speakers in their sex-ed classes. Other districts recognize their own lack of expertise and invite speakers to fill the gap. The Department of Health may be scheduled on one day, Planned Parenthood on another, people from the hospital and the sex crimes division of law enforcement on a third day, and even representatives from PFLAG (Parents and Friends of Lesbians and Gays) on yet another day. Some schools will schedule AIDS patients; others will invite young women who have experienced an abortion, who are placing a child for adoption, or who are single parenting.

Some of these speakers will no doubt present values with which you do not agree. Be careful; find out what viewpoints will be expressed. If your child does attend a controversial talk, you'll want to know what was said so that you can discuss it afterward.

Some parents may decide not to allow their child to hear a representative from Planned Parenthood or PFLAG; the challenge is that this won't prevent your child from talking with other kids in the class about what was said.

Your best prevention is to know what's going on, to know who's doing the talking, and to discuss it with your child.

How to Determine If Your School's Sex-Education Curriculum Effectively Teaches True Abstinence

Comprehensive, character-based human sexuality education will:[2]

- Hold up abstinence as the golden standard (not merely as a lifestyle option equal to being sexually active)
- Continuously stress abstinence when issues of STDs, AIDS, and contraceptive methods are discussed
- Encourage parental involvement in curriculum decisions and student assignments
- Not strive for "neutrality" when discussing life choices, but rather teach that students must learn to discern between good and poor choices
- Be based on respect for the whole individual, their capabilities and experiences (not based on fear)
- Be value-oriented toward temperance, prudence, and chastity
- Believe abstinence is a realistic, attainable goal for teenagers

- Address the biology of reproduction
- Use statistics from reliable sources (such as the Center for Disease Control or the Food and Drug Administration)
- Structure role-playing for students to practice target behaviors
- Discourage teen parenthood
- Promote marriage and monogamy
- Promote the unique contribution of both the father's and the mother's role in childrearing
- Encourage healthy dating relationships
- Discuss physical, emotional, mental, and social aspects of early sexual involvement
- Educate to the appropriate cognitive level of students

Opting Out

If you choose to pull your child out of sex-ed class, you risk both ostracizing him and exposing him to the information secondhand from peers. Whether your kid is in the class or not, if it is held during an hour when you can be there, be there. Teachers should be open to including parents in the loop. If there is ever a time you are *not* allowed in the classroom, be highly suspicious.

There may be occasions, however, when you decide to have your kid skip the class. While few kids are thrilled to talk about penises and vaginas with their peers, some may not be developmentally ready for the material. Perhaps they've simply grown up much more slowly than other kids. Or maybe they've been violated in some way; perhaps they've seen something or had something done to them. If your kid reacts strongly to the class and you feel this suggests some core violation, then don't ignore his or her protective mechanisms. Find out what's going on.

If you believe your child falls into one of these categories, that doesn't mean you should "skip" the material; you can still discuss the basic issues at home or choose to attend the class together.

What to Do If Your Child Is Already Sexually Active

Grace's mom, Margaret, felt as mortified as her daughter when both discovered that Grace had a reputation as "that girl on the back of the bus." Grace, an early adolescent, had been exchanging oral sex with boys in the back of the school bus and sneaking out at night to do the train game (as obscene as it sounds). When her parents came to Kathy, Grace felt horrified that she was gaining a reputation as "a whore."

To Grace, it had all been in fun. But now that she realized the consequences, she was full of regret. "I don't even know why I did it, Mrs. Bell. I have no idea why. I just looked around and everybody else was doing it. Nobody was getting hurt."

"Today is a turning point," I told Grace. "You're not 'that girl on the back of the bus' anymore."

Fortunately, Grace's story has a happy ending; she made some significant changes, which we'll talk about later.

What can you do if you suddenly discover that your son or daughter has a reputation?

Twenty-four Hours

Your son or daughter needs to see that the situation they've gotten themselves into is serious. You need to create a sense of urgency and expectancy. We recommend that you try to make the first twenty-four hours after your discovery a day of intense and active mobilization.

First, you'll need to create a support team: Who is going to help your kid with the new patterns you're setting up? Who is going to support *you?* Sure, you're going to talk with those closest to you, but you will also need help finding answers to questions out of your league: a pastor, rabbi, or priest to talk about spiritual values; a counselor to help you sort through your own issues that may surface as you talk with your child about his or her sexuality; a family physician to answer medical questions and help support you on physical health and hygiene. And initially you're going to have to do much of this without your kid knowing about it.

Next, you're going to need to make several appointments and keep them. You'll visit the pastor, a counselor, a physician, maybe a teacher or the parents of the child your son or daughter is seeing. You'll need to discuss how best (and when and where) to approach your child.

Though all this may seem like a whirlwind, it will help create that turning-point feeling for your child: things are going to be different from here on out. We highly recommend taking time off work at least for this initial day. You need to focus on your family.

Keep in mind that changing the patterns of a seventh grader is going to be very different from changing those of a fourth grader. In fact, for the fourth grader, added time together is probably going to be welcomed. A seventh or eighth grader, however, will be wondering why you are suddenly elbowing into their life. The older your kids are, the more difficult it will be.

Create a Supportive and United Front

How's your marriage? Are you making decisions together? You need a united front. If you begin waving the banner of abstinence *after* your teen already has been sexually active, you will have to give your kids *stellar* reasons to wait—and first and foremost on the list will be your own marriage. It's okay if you and your spouse don't have everything together in your relationship, but you will need to be honest with your kid about your commitment to one another if strain exists.

Children today are intensely attuned to hypocrisy. If you or your spouse has been unfaithful, we'll be honest: you're going to have a difficult time convincing them of why *they* should be sexually responsible.

In addition to the united front of you and your spouse, you need to create a united front with anyone who has any responsibility for your child. For instance, if someone picks your kid up from school, make sure it's someone who supports your value system. You need someone who won't take, "Oh, I've got to study for a test after school with Angie. I'll wait until the last bus or I'll get a ride home." You need people strong enough to stick to the plan if you can't be there, someone who will say, "No, sweetheart, you're coming home with me. Those are the rules."

Be Honest about Your Shortcomings

There is no substitute for honest, authentic relationships. What has kept you from having the relationship you want with your kid, the areas that you feel you'd do over again if you could? Write these on an index card. Then literally lay the cards on the table together with your spouse. What can you realistically change in your relationship with your kid?

Begin with an apology. Own up to your mistakes and shortcomings. Tell your child that you, too, are eager to change, that you hope you'll all come out of this process as better people.

Be encouraged: it's never too late to begin building a track record, though starting late certainly won't be without difficulties. An apology will usually help knock down your child's defenses; most kids will say, "An apology? For what?"

Your kid may react negatively when she realizes what you have in mind to talk about, but that's when you need to stand up and say, "Well, honey, I hear what you're saying, but there *are* some things we need to talk about." Then maintain a determined attitude that you are going to talk.

Talk Openly about Sex—*Very* Openly

Once your child is sexually active, you don't have a choice; you must talk openly about sex. You'll do more harm by trying to pull your kid back to some sense of naïveté when she's already experienced sex. You've got to talk about diseases, about the dangers of oral sex, about the implications of various forms of sexual activity.

What your child needs now is frank, honest, and open discussion. "I understand how this could happen," you might say, "because sex *is* such a powerful force. I don't love you any less; I love you just as much. My love for you does not diminish. But I hope for your sake that you're going to be able to stop this, because this isn't good for you. We're here to help you in whatever way we can."

More than ever, your kid needs to be your hero. You can't shame her back into abstinence. You will push your child the opposite way if you berate her or resort to name-calling. Stay close to your kid, and don't be punitive. Give informed guidance, express your belief that he or she can succeed, and offer unqualified, unconditional love.

Doctor's Appointment

You'll need to contact your kid's physician to talk about Susie Q's situation without her being in the room. You'll also need to schedule a physical and STD check. Brief the physician over the phone or alone in person, because you will probably not be in the examination room with your child when the exam happens. Make sure that your physician will support you on your values, whatever decisions you make. If you are setting boundaries for abstinent behavior, you don't want your doctor handing her condoms and telling her how to use them. If you're not united as parent and physician, it will create additional problems.

The medical exam has two purposes: (1) you really do want to make sure she hasn't caught a disease, and (2) you want her to understand how serious the consequences are of what she's doing. She is risking a lot by becoming sexually active. A girl is likely to think twice while a doctor examines her genitalia; for boys, those STD checks involve inserting what looks like a mascara brush a couple of inches down the urethra. It's not a fun outing!

After what will be a somewhat traumatic experience, your child will certainly need emotional support. This isn't the time for a lengthy or scolding lecture. Let their unpleasant experience be their teacher during this time.

Counseling Appointment

You'll need to set up time with a family counselor. Don't be tempted to try to solve *all* your problems; you need to be very focused on your goals and on what you hope to accomplish *right now*. There will be plenty of time to deal with other issues later.

Be very specific with your counselor. Ask where to go for outside help: books, toll-free numbers, churches with great youth groups. Find out all you can to set your child up for success, knowing that it will take time for your child to establish new patterns.

Talk with the Other Parents

Do your best to get to know the parents of the boy your daughter is involved with. Sit down and talk with them. If you can get them to cooperate, all the better.

All you can do in this area is give it your best shot. The other parents may not care about what's happening; but if that's the case, if it were one of our daughters, she certainly wouldn't ever set foot in that boy's house again. Sure, she may not like us for a while, but then that's never our ultimate goal as parents.

Find Alternative Activities

If you're pulling in the reins and saying to your daughter, "Look, you're not going to be dating Joe anymore," what will she do with her time? Joe very likely may still pursue her, and she's still going to sense a "need" for him. If you're not putting something in Joe's place that you're committed to for the next few years, Susie Q is going to find a way to sneak out. What can you set up for her on Friday night?

Find a volunteer opportunity, an internship, something that taps into her strengths and makes her shine. You may have to give up your own social life for your family during this time. We know of one father who walked into his job the day after finding out that his child was sexually active and quit his role as pastor of a large church.

How far are you willing to go to take care of your kid's needs?

Be Suspicious of Radical or Sudden Change in Behavior

"Is this a *radical* change in behavior?" I (Kathy) asked one mother who told me that her daughter had very unexpectedly become sexually active in the last year.

Discovering your child's sexual activity probably will always come as somewhat of a shock, but when I hear parents say certain sexualized behavior is a "radical change," completely unexpected and against family values, I immediately wonder whether something traumatic happened. Did a friend or family member die? Are the parents getting a divorce? If you can't connect the dots to this sexual behavior, is it possible that he or she was raped or molested?

When change is radical or sudden, it's very likely that something pivotal happened to lead your daughter to seek consolation in the arms of boys.

Naturally, the woman to whom I asked this question at first felt great shock; she'd never considered such possibilities. But as she thought back over the previous year for anything out of the ordinary, she recalled a trip her daughter had taken to Mexico with her cousin. "But I don't remember her saying anything happened there," she added.

"I want you to go to your daughter and ask what happened," I said. "But before you do, you need to get your support team ready. Who's your pastor? Let him know you're doing this. Do you have a counselor? You need to prepare your support so that you, in turn, are ready to support your daughter during this time."

When this mother saw me a week later, she melted into tears. Her daughter and her daughter's cousin had been on the beach in Mexico when a group of guys approached them and began talking. The girls flirted with them a bit and were about to walk away, but the boys chased after them, and her daughter was raped. Because the daughter had flirted with them, she believed she was responsible, so she had kept it a secret.

"I could not believe it," the mother said. "Kathy, what do I do now?"

I said, "You go to your support team that we talked about, beginning with getting her to a doctor as soon as possible."

"No!" she cried.

"You've got no choice," I said. "She's got to get tested for AIDS and other STDs. She needs you now more than ever."

Pray

Situations such as these remind us of the central importance of prayer during crises. Pray for people in your path and in your child's path, for God to hem your child in, for grace, mercy, and knowledge as you take steps through this time. Above all, remember that nothing can separate *you* and your family from the love of God, who is with you every step of the way as you minister his love to your child.

Secondary Virginity

There is a growing movement among kids who have been sexually active and then pledge to remain abstinent until marriage; it's called secondary virginity. Kids need to know that we all make mistakes and that there is indeed forgiveness and healing.

Unfortunately, all good intentions for secondary virginity often end up as "momentary" virginity if they move too quickly without doing some inner work. Just because we know we shouldn't eat donuts doesn't mean we're not going to eat them; donuts taste good. Many times, people who "go off the wagon" and then return to their previous behavior do worse because, in their mind, they've already blown it, so what's the difference?

There is hope, but change has to come from within your child, and a lot has to happen inside a person for that change to stick. St. Paul said it best when he regretted behaviors in his life he didn't want to do but found himself doing anyway (see Romans 7:19). Guilt is probably going to play a role in propelling a sexually active child to pledge abstinence, and a certain amount of guilt is not such a bad thing. But that commitment to secondary virginity doesn't mean much if guilt is all you're running on.

We've both counseled many kids and young women for whom a significant part of their foundation is missing—that of a loving dad for a young girl, for example. That girl must acknowledge the void and be vigilant that she doesn't again put herself in a position in her relationships where she compromises herself to grasp for the attention of men.

That's why we mention the role of a counselor and/or pastor in your support team. It's not enough for your child to say "No." You have to give your kid something else to say yes to.

The good news is that your child can change. God is a forgiving, loving, and healing God. Ask him to help provide motivation.

Remember Grace? Kathy got together with "that girl from the back of the bus" after she and her parents had passed through the first twenty-four hours.

"Did you talk to every single person on that list?" I asked Grace.

"Yes," she said. "I've scheduled meetings with all of them, and I know I have to change my reputation and bring my grades up." She pointed out where she had failed and recognized at what points her team had agreed to support her.

"Now, what are we going to do when you go back to school and people tease you?" I asked Grace.

"I will have to deal with it."

"Yes, unfortunately, you will. But *how* will you deal with it?"

We talked about how Grace could fortify herself internally by reminding herself of the positive changes she was making. We also talked about establishing a new group of friends.

"What skill will you need," I asked her, "when you're in situations that push your boundaries? How will you turn around, back up, say no? Do you need a buddy by you all the time? What's your worst hour? Can we change your lunch hour? Can you find a teacher who will help you?"

These are the types of questions you'll need to ask your child as you seek to effect long-term change. The first twenty-four hours are a crucial start, but they are still only the first step of a long journey.

Notes

Chapter 1
1. Josh McDowell, *Right from Wrong* (Dallas: Word, 1994), 268.
2. Term used by Dr. Mary Manz Simon in her book *How to Parent Your "Tweenager."*
3. Editor, "1994 All-USA High-School USA Today Baseball Team," *USA Today*, 21 June 1994, C6.

Chapter 2
1. Jack O. and Judith K. Balswick, *The Family: A Christian Perspective on the Contemporary Home* (Grand Rapids: Baker), 98.
2. Michelle Burford, "Girls and Sex: You Won't Believe What's Going On," *O* magazine (November 2002): 214–15.

Chapter 3
1. "They Said It," *Sports Illustrated*, 26 November 2001, 36.
2. Our account of this period of Jason Kidd's life is based on S. L. Price, "A Clean Start," *Sports Illustrated*, 28 January 2002, 58–70.

Chapter 4
1. Evgenia Peretz, "Born to Be Wild," *Vanity Fair*, November 2001, 186.
2. Ibid., 191.
3. Ibid.
4. Ibid., 200.
5. Chris Tauber, "Priced Out of the Prom," *New York Times Upfront*, 5 March 2001, 18–19.
6. Kaiser Family Foundation, Sex on TV 2: A Biennial Report to the Kaiser Family Foundation—Executive Summary, (Menlo Park, Calif.: The Henry J. Kaiser Family Foundation, 2001), 2.
7. SIECUS, "Teens and TV," (2001, vol. 1, issue 2, supplement: Families Are Talking), 2. Statistic taken from 2001 Kaiser Family Foundation and Seventeen Survey of Teens: "Teen's Opinions, Attitudes, and Awareness of Sexually Transmitted Diseases."
8. Michael D. Lemonick, "Teens Before Their Time," *Time*, 30 October 2000, 74.

Chapter 5
1. This account is based on Michael Bamberger, "New York Firefighters," *Sports Illustrated*, 24 December 2001, 108.

2. Lorraine Ali and Julie Scelfo, "Choosing Virginity," *Newsweek*, 9 December 2002, 64.
3. Martin Perlman, "Wear Your Helmet, Go Get Free Ice Cream," *Washington Health Today*, fall 2001. Washington Health Foundation: www.whf.org/newsletters/Today/Archives/Fall%20Web%20Pages/Fall2 001sec8.htm.
4. Ben Cohen and Jerry Greenfield, *Ben & Jerry's Double Dip: Lead with Your Values and Make Money, Too* (New York: Simon & Schuster, 1997), 13.
5. Ibid., 15–16.
6. Ben & Jerry's website: www.benjerry.com/co-index.tmpl/about_us/.
7. Bamberger, "New York Firefighters," 108.

Chapter 7
1. Robert Hardman, "Edward and Sophie: A Royal Wedding Celebration," Telegraph online, 21 June 1999, www.telegraph.co.uk.
2. See "Brad and Jennifer Tie the Knot," BBC News online, 30 July 2000, news.bbc.co.uk/1/hi/entertainment/858367.stm; Simon Davis, "Brad Pitt's $1m Wedding Ring of Steel," Telegraph online, 31 July 2000, www.telegraph.co.uk/news/main.jhtml?xml=/news/2000/07/31/wedd3 1.xml; and Camerin Courtney, "Star Gazing," ChristianityToday.com, 9 August 2000, www.christianitytoday.com/singles/newsletter/mind 00809.html.
3. BBC's website: news.bbc.co.uk/onthisday/hi/dates/stories/july/29/ newsid_2494000/2494949.stm.
4. BBC's website: news.bbc.co.uk/1/hi/uk/249775.stm.
5. Historic Royal Palaces' website: www.hrp.org.uk/webcode/content .asp?ID=542.
6. Yolanda Woodee, "Black Fashion Museum Mostly a Site Unseen," *Washington Post*, 13 March 2003, T25.
7. Loren Cordain et. al., "Acne Vulgaris: A Disease of Western Civilization," Archives of Dermatology online, 2002, 138:1584–1590. Website: archderm.ama-assn.org/.
8. www.hygieneconcepts.com.

Chapter 8
1. Lemonick, "Teens Before Their Time," 74.
2. Lakita Garth, "Beauty Queen," *We Can Make a Difference* (Tucson: fall 2002), 16.
3. Kelly Brownell, a Yale psychology professor, came up with these calculations in the year 2000.

4. Paul Donohue, "To Your Health: Breast Growth Embarrasses Boy," *Columbian*, 20 January 2000, E3.
5. Michael Gurian, *The Wonder of Girls* (New York: Pocket Books, 2002), 39–40.
6. Greg Botelho, "Inspired into Action: Teenager an Advocate for Youths Making a Difference in the World," CNNfyi.com, 10 September 2000, CNN's website: CNNfyi.com, www.cnn.com/2000/fyi/real.life/09/12/amber.coffman/.

Chapter 12
1. Anna Mulrine, "Risky Business: Teens Are Having More Sex—and Getting More Diseases. But Is Telling Them to Wait the Answer?" *U.S. News and World Report*, 27 May 2002, 42–44.
2. Ibid., 45–46.
3. Jodie Morse, "An Rx for Teen Sex" *Time*, 7 October 2002, 65.
4. Ali and Scelfo, "Choosing Virginity," 66.
5. Q & A Kids' Questions—Parents' Answers (National Physicians Center for Family Resources), 33, quoting The Cautious Generation? Teens Tell Us about Sex, Virginity and "the Talk" (National Campaign to Prevent Teen Pregnancy: April 2000).
6. Virginia de Leon, "Group Helps Teenagers Choose Abstinence. Spokane High School Program May Be Unique in Nation," *Spokesman Review*, 14 October 2000, B1.
7. Desda Moss, "Parental Worry #184: Teen Sex at Home," USAToday.com, 10 October 2002, www.usatoday.com/news/opinion/editorials/2002–10 –10-opcom_x.htm.
8. Associated Press, "Teens Most Likely to Have Sex at Home," USAToday.com, 26 September 2002, www.usatoday.com/news/health/2002–09–26-teen-sex_x.htm.
9. Kaiser Family Foundation, quoted in *Time*, 18 February 2002, 78.
10. Philip Elmer-Dewitt, "Now for the Truth about Americans and Sex," *Time*, 17 October 1994, 64.
11. Robert T. Michael et. al., *Sex in America: A Definitive Survey* (Boston: Little, Brown and Company, 1994), 124.
12. "Now for the Truth about Americans and Sex," 68.

Appendix 1
1. The Medical Institute for Sexual Health's website: www.medinstitute .org/.
2. Shannon Federoff, chastity educator, Youth Sexuality Program, 1998.

Recommended Resources

The Educated Child by William Bennett

> Answers questions such as: Is your child getting what he should out of school? What should you be looking for in a school? What should you expect or even demand from your school? and What is essential in K–8?

The Hurried Child, Growing Up Too Fast, Too Soon by Dr. David Elkind

> By blurring the boundaries of what is age-appropriate, by expecting or imposing too much too soon, we force our kids to grow up too fast, to mimic adult sophistication while secretly yearning for innocence.

Good Families Don't Just Happen by Catherine Musco Garcia-Prats and Joseph A. Garcia-Prats, M.D.

> The authors are parents of ten well-mannered children and discuss their principles for nurturing good families. The Garcia-Prats family and their book were featured on the *Oprah* show.

Adolescence Isn't Terminal: It Just Feels Like It! by Dr. Kevin Leman

> Dr. Leman discusses how to relate to and grow closer to your adolescent child.

What a Difference a Daddy Makes by Dr. Kevin Leman

> Discusses the crucial role that fathers play in the lives of their daughters.

First-Time Mom by Dr. Kevin Leman.

> A comprehensive, practical guide to raising your child for the first-time mom.

Why Wait? by Josh McDowell

> Discusses psychological, physical, emotional, and spiritual reasons to wait for marriage to have sex.

Saving Childhood: Protecting Our Children from the National Assault on Innocence by Michael and Diane Medved

> Children today are unnecessarily fearful, cynical, and sad. This book discusses how to maintain a child's innocence for its proper duration by providing psychological security, encouraging children's sense of wonder, and inculcating optimism.

But I Love Him by Dr. Jill Murray

> Helps you show your teen what a respectful relationship looks like and teach her the importance of respecting herself.

Sex Smart: 501 Reasons to Hold Off on Sex by Susan Browning Pogany

> Straightforward answers to hundreds of questions teens have about sex and relationships.

The Net-Mom's Internet Kids and Family Yellow Pages by Jean Armour Polly

> Polly, professional librarian and mom, explores the internet to find the best, most engaging, and most fun websites ever. More than 3,500 handpicked, kid-safe websites.

Parenthood by Proxy: Don't Have Them if You Won't Raise Them by Dr. Laura Schlessinger

> Dr. Laura takes on American parenting practices.

A Return to Modesty: Discovering the Lost Virtue by Wendy Shalit

> Probes the cultural history of sexual modesty for women and considers whether this virtue may be beneficial in today's world.

The Unexpected Legacy of Divorce, a 25-Year Landmark Study by Judith Wallerstein

> A million new children a year are added to our march of marital failures. See what is happening to our lives.

National Guidelines for Sexuality and Character Education booklet
Abstinence vs. "Safer Sex" Sexuality Education Comparison booklet

> The Medical Institute for Sexual Health is an excellent organization that presents character-based sexuality education. To order these booklets, call 1-800-892-9484, or visit www.medinstitute.org.

Index

For information regarding speaking availability, business consultations, or seminars, please contact Dr. Leman at:

Dr. Kevin Leman
P.O. Box 35370
Tucson, Arizona 85740
Phone (520) 797-3830
Fax (520) 797-3809
Websites:
    www.realfamilies.com
    www.matchwise.com
    www.drleman.com

Books by Dr. Kevin Leman

Winning the Rat Race without Becoming a Rat
The Birth Order Book
Making Children Mind without Losing Yours
First Time Mom
A Chicken's Guide to Talking Turkey with Your Kids about Sex
The Way of the Shepherd
Sex Begins in the Kitchen
The Perfect Match
Sheet Music—Uncovering the Secrets of Sexual Intimacy in Marriage
When Your Best Is Not Good Enough
Women Who Try Too Hard
Becoming the Parent God Wants You to Be
Becoming a Couple of Promise
Living in a Stepfamily without Getting Stepped On
What a Difference a Daddy Makes
Making Sense of the Men in Your Life
Say Goodbye to Stress
The Real You—Becoming the Person You Were Meant to Be
Unlocking the Secrets of Your Childhood Memories
Keeping Your Family Strong in a World Gone Wrong
Ten Secrets to Raising Sensible, Successful Kids
My Firstborn, There's No One Like You
My Middle Child, There's No One Like You
My Lastborn, There's No One Like You
My Only Child, There's No One Like You

Audiotapes

Why Kids Misbehave and What You Can Do about It
How to Make Your Child Feel Special
Keeping Your Family Together When the World Is Falling Apart
Living in a Stepfamily without Getting Stepped On

Videotapes

Raising Successful and Confident Kids
How to Get Kids to Do What You Want
Why Kids Misbehave and What You Can Do about It
Living in a Stepfamily without Getting Stepped On

Video Series (with study guide, DVD, and audiotape)

Making Children Mind without Losing Yours (Christian parenting edition)
Making Children Mind without Losing Yours (public-school edition)
Making the Most of Marriage
Single Parenting That Works!
Bringing Peace and Harmony to the Blended Family

Dr. Kevin Leman

"Practical Wisdom with a Smile"

Founder of www.matchwise.com, internationally known Christian psychologist, award-winning author, radio and television personality, and speaker, Dr. Kevin Leman has ministered to and entertained audiences worldwide with his wit and common-sense psychology.

Bestselling author Dr. Leman has made house calls for Focus on the Family with Dr. James Dobson, as well as numerous radio and television programs including *Oprah*, *Live with Regis and Kelly*, CBS's *The Early Show*, *Today*, and *The View with Barbara Walters*. Dr. Leman is a frequent contributor to CNN's *American Morning*. Dr. Leman has served as a consulting family psychologist to *Good Morning America*.

Dr. Leman is founder and president of Couples of Promise, an organization designed for and committed to helping couples remain happily married.

Dr. Leman's professional affiliations include the American Psychological Association, American Federation of Radio and Television Artists, National Register of Health Services Providers in Psychology, and the North American Society of Adlerian Psychology.

Dr. Leman attended North Park College. He received his bachelor's degree in psychology from the University of Arizona, where he later earned his master's and doctorate degrees. Originally from Williamsville, New York, he and his wife, Sande, live in Tucson. They have five children and one grandchild.

More Information about Kathy Bell and Helpful Websites

1. Kathy's website

www.kitchentablesexed.com

With links to Kathy's favorite abstinence educators and educators within her programs in Tucson

2. WAIT (Why Am I Tempted) Training

Joneen Krauth, RN, and Shelly Donahue, National Trainer
Abstinence and Relationship Training Center
2938 Cottesford Way
Smyrna, GA 30080
Phone: 770-333-1780
Fax: 770-333-1798
Email: nationalabstinencetc@earthlink.net

3. Choosing the Best, Inc.

Bruce and Donna Cook
2625 Cumberland Parkway, Ste 200
Atlanta, GA 30339
Phone: 770-803-3100
          800-774-2378
Fax: 770-803-3110
Email: www.choosingthebest.org

4. Hygiene Concepts

www.hygieneconcepts.com

Hygiene Educator and Licensed Cosmotologist

Specializes in training children ages third grade and up in proper hygiene, product respect and maintenance

5. Body Image Educator

Specializes in eating disorders, disordered eating, and body image education for ages third grade and up

Joyce Mann, MSW

BodyImageGuide@Mindspring.com

Share Your Thoughts

With the Author: Your comments will be forwarded to
the author when you send them to *zauthor@zondervan.com*.

With Zondervan: Submit your review of this book
by writing to *zreview@zondervan.com*.

Free Online Resources at

www.zondervan.com/hello

 Zondervan AuthorTracker: Be notified whenever your
favorite authors publish new books, go on tour, or post
an update about what's happening in their lives.

 Daily Bible Verses and Devotions: Enrich your life
with daily Bible verses or devotions that help you start
every morning focused on God.

 Free Email Publications: Sign up for newsletters on
fiction, Christian living, church ministry, parenting, and
more.

 Zondervan Bible Search: Find and compare
Bible passages in a variety of translations at
www.zondervanbiblesearch.com.

 Other Benefits: Register yourself to receive online
benefits like coupons and special offers, or to participate
in research.